100+ IDEAS
FOR MANAGING BEHAVIOUR

CONTINUUM ONE HUNDREDS SERIES

100+ IDEAS
FOR MANAGING
BEHAVIOUR

Johnnie Young

continuum

*This book is dedicated to my wife Sylvie
and my three children Edward, Julie and William.
They have been with me all the way.*

Continuum International Publishing Group

The Tower Building   80 Maiden Lane, Suite 704
11 York Road   New York
London   NY 10038
SE1 7NX

www.continuumbooks.com

© Johnnie Young 2007

All rights reserved. No part of this publication may be
reproduced or transmitted in any form or by any means,
electronic or mechanical, including photocopying, recording,
or any information storage or retrieval system, without prior
permission in writing from the publishers.

Johnnie Young has asserted his right under the Copyright, Designs
and Patents Act, 1988, to be identified as Author of this work.

British Library Cataloguing-in-Publication Data
A catalogue record for this book is available from the British
Library.

ISBN: 0826493165 (paperback)

Library of Congress Cataloging-in-Publication Data
A catalog record for this book is available from the Library
of Congress

Typeset by Ben Cracknell Studios | www.benstudios.co.uk
Printed and bound in Great Britain by Ashford Colour Press,
Gosport, Hampshire

CONTENTS

SECTION 4 Dealing with common problems

SECTION 7 **Managing yourself**

ACKNOWLEDGEMENTS

First of all I would like to thank my publishers, Continuum, and in particular Alexandra Webster for her vision in seeing the potential of my original idea and Christina Garbutt who has been wonderful in her guidance, patience and support all along the way.

There are dozens of teachers who, over the years, have taught me so much. I would like to thank my friend and colleague William Barnard for his indispensable advice and support. I would like to thank John Holt for believing in me. Bob Pennifold is a genius, unforgettable and a much-loved inspiration to me and many others (particularly students with challenging behaviour!). David Pryke taught me when I was a student and became a colleague and great friend. Thank you. I would like also to thank Jayne Blenkarn, the best head of department and the hardest worker I know. From the teachers of the distant past who taught me when I was a student I would like to thank Tony Ranson for inspiring me in English, Chris Young (no relation) for inspiring me in drama, my brother Derek who taught me to read in the early days, my brother Brian who is a natural and clear communicator and last of all, the greatest teacher I ever knew, my mother, for inspiring me in life! Thank you all.

INTRODUCTION

I started teaching straight after leaving a management position in a bank. I had been with the bank for sixteen years but had dreamed of being a teacher all my life. I wanted to influence a whole generation of students. I had studied part-time to get an Open University Honours Degree in English Literature; had taught staff in the bank; and had held evening adult education classes for some time. So with confidence I strode into my first school who had kindly agreed to try me out on an unqualified basis.

And so it was that I was led to my first classroom where a Year 9 middle-ability class waited. 'Today we're going to study a poem,' I importantly announced to the class. 'What's a poem?' came a shouted reply. The next hour was the worst of my life. All I could think was: 'What have I done?' I started training to become a 'licensed teacher'. I attended university once a week for two years and was observed in my classroom environment on countless occasions.

My lessons were, quite frankly, a battleground. True, I knew my subject. I knew it well. But the problem was I didn't know how to teach it. The classes were bored with me. I shouted all lesson. I gave handfuls of detention slips. I ended each lesson exhausted and depressed. I started considering a completely different line of work. I really didn't know what to do.

I realized that when I observed lessons of experienced teachers some seemed to do much better than others. I began asking these teachers lots of questions and I recorded their answers in a notebook (this was to be the first of many notebooks). I realized I thought I knew how to teach, but I really would have to start from scratch. I made it a habit to record helpful tips from experienced teachers. 'What do you do if they want to go to the toilet?' I would ask. 'If you let one go they all want to go. If you say no they might wee themselves.' 'Tell them to wait ten minutes and if it's still an emergency let them go,' came the reply. Into my notebook it went.

Over the years I filled dozens of notebooks with thousands of ideas. I still do. That is the great thing about teaching. You never stop learning. As I became more experienced I started to come up with my own ideas and adapted old ones. If I had a particularly good lesson I would reflect on why it was good. I noted down the essence of the reason why.

I have noticed, with regret, that a lot of staff in education have given up the ghost and left the profession feeling disillusioned. I have been teaching now for twelve years. I didn't leave because I realized that like any craft there is a knack to doing it. I have not always had brilliant lessons. No teacher can ever claim that. But as I've learnt more about the craft of teaching and tried to put the ideas into practice I have enjoyed the experience more and more, and I think my students have too.

I have extracted the best 120 ideas from my notebooks for dealing with students with challenging behaviour. When I began teaching I wish I could have got my hands on a book which gave practical tips on how to teach more effectively. I used to despair at the thickly laid academic texts that seemed to bear no relation to the classroom experience. This is why I've turned my ideas into this book to help new, and I hope experienced, teachers. The beauty of these ideas is that they are all tried and tested in a classroom environment. Some include actual examples of the words a teacher may use in a particular situation. There are comments designed to make teachers aware of risk areas and there are many strategies offered for teaching students with challenging behaviour.

I hope that in a small way my book will inspire teachers to give the best of themselves and to get the best from their students. Here it is. I hope you like it.

Johnnie Young

Getting to know them . . .

KNOWING THEIR NAMES

The first few lessons with a challenging class can be extremely difficult as you struggle, under pressure, to learn your students' names. To learn their names quickly try one or all of the following:

○ Seat them alphabetically as they appear in the register.
○ Ask them to make simple signs out of A4 paper with their name clearly written on. They should keep this in front of them until you're confident as to who's who.
○ Ask them to bring in passport photographs of themselves which you stick to a seating plan next to their names.

If these are students in Year 8 or upwards it's useful to talk to teachers who taught them in previous years. They may have useful advice on how to deal with particularly difficult students or classes.

Build up a profile of your students' interests. It will take time and patience but persevere because it's an investment that will pay huge dividends.

If, for example, they have to write a story, students will often complain they can't think what to write about. In response the teacher may suggest several options, none of which inspires the student. How much better to be able to say:

> *'Imagine you're fishing (you know the student loves fishing) and you catch a huge one. When you reel it in you are amazed at what you find . . . Continue the story . . . '*

You will find that this is much more effective than a blanket 'write about anything' approach.

KNOWING YOUR STUDENTS' INTERESTS

USING THEIR LIFE TARGETS TO MOTIVATE

Following on from Idea 2, keep building a profile of each student and gradually you'll get a picture of what they want to do in life. This information is very useful as you can raise students' interest levels by linking the subject matter to their personal interests.

For example, you're trying to teach an uninterested student how to produce a colour chart in an art lesson. If you know he or she wants to be a hairdresser you can ask him or her to design a chart of different hair colours, or to design the colours into different hairstyles.

In practice it's not, of course, possible to do this sort of thing with every student in every lesson. However, as part of your 'toolkit' to tackle certain problems it can be a wonderful way to motivate students into doing good, meaningful work.

Students with challenging behaviour often have low self-esteem and little regard for the value and worth of their work.

When a student produces work it's important to be honest and specific about how it could be improved. Remember to always show that you value his or her efforts and point out something that's been done well. You may be the only person in that student's life who has the chance to give positive feedback.

At first you may come up against certain students who disbelieve your apparent appreciation of their work. Don't give up! Appreciate every improvement no matter how small. Show students how they're improving by comparing work done now to work from several weeks ago. In time you will win over their trust and your comments will be important to them. This is a long, hard process and they'll know if you're not sincere.

Finally, remember that however badly a lesson goes, next lesson spring back and be enthusiastic about their work again. They will soon get used to your indomitable style!

ELEVATING THE IMPORTANCE OF STUDENTS' WORK

A great way of dealing with students and creating a better classroom atmosphere is to use humour. However, there are two things you should be careful of.

1 Don't use humour until you're confident you have control over the class. Misplaced humour can cause the very trouble you were seeking to avoid.

2 Be aware that although it may not show, particularly with badly behaved students, they're at a very sensitive and self-conscious age. A comment designed to create a harmless giggle at the size of a student's nose could have a really disastrous set of consequences.

Safer ground is to never make a personal comment about a student, even in jest, and to stick to either making fun of yourself or the topic you're studying. Once you've made a joke try and get the class back to the task at hand as soon as possible.

There is a tendency, particularly with new teachers, to be too friendly with students. When adults interact they do so in a friendly manner to ensure smooth relationships. It's natural to assume that by being friendly to students you'll get the best out of them. But be careful. You are not a friend to the student: you're their teacher. One of your most important roles is to lead and organize their learning environment. If you are too friendly many students will not do as you ask them, and with challenging students this can become a disaster.

The main tip here is to think long term. It's not just one lesson you need to think about. You're attempting to build a long-term relationship where each time you meet the student you help them progress in their learning. If you're too strict you risk coming up against confrontation straight away. If you're too friendly the students will see you as a soft touch.

It's best, therefore, to work out your own rules of engagement. Develop your individual classroom personality and try and pitch it between the two extremes mentioned above. Always be consistent with your approach. Once the students are familiar with your rules of engagement they will work within them and know when they step outside of them. The students prefer this because they know clearly where they stand and what to expect from you.

FRIEND OR FOE?

YOUR ATTITUDE HELPS

If you listen to comments made by students about teachers they don't like you often hear this: 'He's miserable.'

If you always have an interested, friendly, upbeat attitude and you are consistent with it (this should all be part of the rules of engagement set up in Idea 6), you will find this has a huge effect on the attitude of your students. You're setting the tone, and you'll need resilience to keep bouncing back with this upbeat feel.

If you feel fed up before a lesson pretend to be happy for about five or ten minutes. A remarkable thing happens: you do become happy.

It is true that actions speak louder than words. As far as you are concerned make sure

○ you look like a professional and that you are dressed smartly, otherwise how can you insist on smart uniforms?
○ that you are at the lesson on time, otherwise how can you tell them they are late?
○ you are well organized, or telling them off for forgetting something loses its effect. Notice that the teachers who are well organized are the ones who manage behaviour best
○ lessons are well prepared and appropriate for their ability
○ that the students know the marking rota for the books. If it is once a week make sure that you stick to that
○ you keep meticulous records so that you can spot missing homework immediately and without argument
○ you keep to your promises of rewards and letters home
○ you always stay calm and cool. Continually show that you are calm and firm, whatever the situation

By being a shining example yourself it gives you a great advantage with behaviour management. You are making the wisdom of actions speaking louder than words work to your advantage. For one thing, it takes just the same energy to be on the ball as it does to be sloppy in your work. In fact, unorganized, sloppy teachers who get angry quickly burn up much more energy by looking for things and arguing with students about missing things. They also find themselves in far too many foreseeable and avoidable conflicts.

STAR OF THE MATCH

A great way to get to know your students and to have some fun in the lesson is to have a 'star of the match' system.

Each lesson tell the students that you're going to pick a 'star', and that there are a range of reasons why an individual may be chosen. It may be an improvement

o in effort;
o in quality of work;
o in attitude to work.

Ask the students how they're progressing with their work and be very encouraging of signs of improvement. You'll find that students compete in order to show you they're doing well.

Announce at the end of the lesson who the star is, and specifically what it is they've done to gain the title. Remind the other students that it could be them next time around. Every lesson a student will be chosen and, human nature being what it is, everyone takes an interest. When it works well the students become keen to offer up suggestions about themselves to gain them the coveted title!

To reinforce what it is you're looking for, maintain a chart on the wall with the names of the stars and the reasons and dates. Of course a student can win more than once.

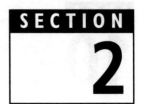

How to keep cool when the going gets tough

THE POWER OF ORGANIZATION

Imagine the situation below.

Sophie demands a pen and starts shouting for one.
She grabs at Henry's who swears back at her.
You search frantically for a spare pen to settle the
argument. You can't find one. While your nose is
buried in your briefcase a fight breaks out. In
desperation you have to lend her your own
expensive pen.

Every teacher has been in a similar situation. The
key to avoiding it is pure and simple: organization.
Try to set aside regular time to plan your
organization in detail. Think out exactly what you'll
need and make a master checklist for each class.
Into each class you should take:

O one case with your master records;
O spare stationery;
O the correct number of worksheets or textbooks;
O anything special for the activities planned.

If you do this life will be easier and you'll increase
the chances of a good, smooth lesson.

Creating an encouraging atmosphere by using positive language is a great habit to get into. For example, instead of saying:

'I told you to be quiet, now I'm getting annoyed!'

You should say:

'Excellent! Most people are becoming quiet. Just a few more and we're there.'

This approach anticipates the results you require and produces a positive atmosphere. You can adapt this to any instructions and any type of behaviour. The tone of the voice may well be firm but the message is saying: 'Good, we're getting there!'

POSITIVE INSTRUCTIONS

IDEA

12

If a teacher has done all they can to get the attention of a class, but the class is still messing about, then it seems natural to start shouting. But what do you do when you shout and the class still takes no notice of you?

When I first started teaching I used to shout a lot and I found that it wore me out and didn't really help much. What was worse was that my voice was damaged and that made the next lesson harder. Over the years I've developed a number of strategies and techniques which remove the need to shout.

○ Stand and wait with a certain 'look'(see Idea 15 for more on this).
○ Lower your voice so that students have to listen harder to hear you.
○ Stop halfway through a sentence or word and glare for a second at the person talking. This is a great method but you must practise to get the timing just right so it doesn't draw a comment from the student.
○ Hold your hand in the air and wait for silence.

The strategic shout also works amazingly well. Try the above techniques first but if somebody is still messing about shout just one word like 'Right!' and then go straight back to your lower voice. This technique protects your voice and, if the strategic shout is correctly timed and directed in the right way, it can work much better than shouting for most of the lesson.

There is a lot of information available about body language and how our own communicates a lot about us. In a classroom, body language and your awareness of it is vital. I have identified some key practical tips below which are useful when it comes to managing challenging behaviour.

Remember that from the moment you enter the classroom you're on show. Thirty pairs of observant eyes are watching and assessing you and they're looking for clues. Are you soft? Are you nervous? Do you know what you're doing? Are you experienced? This is the type of information you are constantly broadcasting with your body language. Remember to:

o look and act confidently;
o stand upright, do not hunch;
o keep your eyes scanning the group;
o show at all times that you're well aware of what is going on by broadcasting your observations;
o develop signals to indicate desired actions (see Idea 14 for more details);
o move about confidently;
o have your records to hand and don't mess around in a briefcase where you cannot watch the class;
o when pointing to the board or visuals be clear and definite;
o have a hotspot where you stand from which you almost always give instructions;
o sometimes stand at the back of the classroom – if a student turns round to see what you're doing point back to their work and continue to stand confidently;
o always be aware of how you move – don't rush or get flustered.

THE IMPORTANCE OF BODY LANGUAGE

IDEA

14

THE BEAUTY OF SIGNALS

Often teachers talk too much and students will not take on board a lot of what's said (although they seem to have developed wonderful ways of looking like they are listening!).

By building up a simple language of symbols, you'll talk less and conserve energy. Here are four examples which have worked well for me.

1 Putting your hand up in the air at the beginning of the lesson, or whenever you require the students to listen, while you hold a prominent finger to your lips is a good way to get them to listen without you having to shout.

2 If a student is not working, point back to his or her book.

3 If a student has not removed a hat or coat, simply mime tugging gently at your own and then point to theirs.

4 A lot of instructions, particularly those which start the lesson can be written on the board, for example: 'Write this title and copy this sentence.'

There are many more examples and you will find the ones that work best for you. The key is to be consistent and to keep the silent signals clear and simple. Use them often and the students will recognize them and cooperate. Apart from anything else, you will ease the strain on your voice!

In the teacher's armoury 'the look' is of great importance. It is a good idea to practise this on your own beforehand. Basically, it's a way of showing, without words, that you're not happy. It works extremely well if you perfect it and use it appropriately, but don't overuse it.

For example, if you're interrupted while explaining something to the class, stop halfway through a sentence and stare at the student responsible. You must get your timing right for this. To stare for too long will invite an unwelcome comment, to stare for too short a time will not have a powerful enough effect. As you look at the student say to yourself, 'one thousand and one, one thousand and two, one thousand and three,' then look away and carry on with what you were saying. I can guarantee that you'll find this is a highly effective technique.

DEVELOPING 'THE LOOK'

THE POWER OF BEING POLITE

When students are impolite to you, you must remain polite, calm and quietly spoken in return. This way, you are constantly reminding the students that:

'I'm being polite to you and I would like you to be polite to me.'

By keeping to these standards you will wear them down with your politeness and they will respect you for it. This ties in with your classroom attitude discussed in Idea 7.

I keep coming back to this because it's so important. Be consistent!

When dealing with students with challenging behaviour, consistency is vital as the students soon get to know if you really do mean what you say. The point of a consistent approach is to decide upon your parameters. Setting unrealistic goals with homework for students with low motivation means they'll never be achieved. Giving too many detentions is exhausting for you to follow up. Too many offers of letters home might be difficult to deliver. Work out reasonable parameters, but then make sure you maintain them, for example:

- ○ when giving sanctions make sure that what you threaten to do you actually carry out;
- ○ if you promise to write a letter home to acknowledge good work then make sure you do it;
- ○ if you have to resort to keeping a student in detention make sure that come what may that student ends up in detention;
- ○ if you're chasing outstanding homework don't give up until you've got it.

Over a period of time a professional consistent approach, where the students see that you never fall down on what you say, will build up a long-term trust and will help you enormously in managing your class.

THE POWER OF CONSISTENCY

BEING GENTLE

When faced with a lot of students with challenging behaviour in one class it's all too easy to become annoyed and angry, especially when your carefully prepared lesson starts to fall apart.

It is a useful tip when under such stress to have a mental trigger word like 'gentle' which will remind you, at the time you most need it, to maintain a calm, gentle and persistent approach. Whatever you do, don't get rattled. If you do, the students (who, don't forget, are experts at rattling teachers) will latch on to that and go for you like hyenas stalking an injured lion!

Pretend to be calm. Say confident things like: 'Good, most of the class are working. I'm pleased with that. Now you girls there, a bit more effort please!' Phrases like this give strong messages around the room that you're confident, calm and in control. Stay gentle and persistent and you will win through.

Some students with challenging behaviour will be very skilful at dragging you into an argument. For example, a student may argue with you and then try to pull in support from his or her friends. A good counterbalance to this is to use 'deflection'. This is where you acknowledge what the student says and then deflect attention straight back on to the work. You may have to do this several times. It is also a good idea to focus attention on to another student who you know is working well.

This is a great tactic as it means you don't ignore the disruptive student but you also don't engage in an argument, which will disrupt the progress of the lesson. If you're careful and persistent with this technique you'll find it can be very useful in keeping the behaviour of the class on track.

USING DEFLECTION

IDEA

20

YOUR REACTIONS

It is really useful to think about your reactions to various problems before they arise. Although it's impossible to run through possible reactions to every situation, below is a list of common problems.

Think about how you would react in each given situation and plan an appropriate response.

○ Late arrival to your class.
○ Notes being passed around.
○ Mobile phones being used.
○ Homework not being delivered on time.
○ Missing pens/pencils/work, etc.

Having your reaction planned will give you a greater sense of confidence and makes you look more on the ball. Keep a brief note in your record book about how you did react to problems as they arose, noting what you did right and how you think you may have handled the situation better. This will help you to plan ahead.

In a tired moment your lesson can be ruined by one comment you haven't thought through. It's very easy to do and can cause lots of trouble. A student will capitalize on this situation and the problem can escalate with other students needing no encouragement to join in with the ensuing mayhem. In your attempt to redirect their attention back to the work you'll find you're swimming against a tide of disruption.

The thing to remember is that a classroom is a stressful environment where you have to have your wits about you. The tip therefore is to get into the habit of thinking about the effect of what you're going to say before you actually say it. It sounds so obvious but it's surprising how often teachers forget to do this.

THE WISDOM OF THINKING TWICE

ROLE REVERSAL

With a particularly challenging student it sometimes is a good idea to change the teacher–student relationship, just for a while. Find out what their passion is. What is it that they are always talking about? Is it a football team, a particular sport, a pop star?

The next step is to have a quiet word with them, perhaps after a lesson. Show a genuine interest in the thing that 'makes them tick' and ask them to teach you about it. Get interested in it. A good way to lead into this is to get them to answer a few simple questions about their subject at first, perhaps in a casual way, and then extend it so that they can have the opportunity to tell you much more. They will be pleased, when the situation is right, to be able to tell you about something they know a lot about. An ideal situation is when you can get to the point where you have regular small conversations where they 'teach' you. The key thing here is to show a genuine interest.

It will enhance your relationship with the student in a meaningful way and good relationships are the bedrock of good behaviour management. You will find that when you try and teach them things they listen that little bit more.

In some cases you may be able to develop it and help them so that they can give a small presentation to the class or to an arranged smaller group.

Below are some excellent phrases I've used with students with challenging behaviour.

○ To get attention, hold up an object and say: 'Can anyone in this room tell me what this is?'
○ To warn about a sanction: 'Right, I don't usually have to do this but you leave me no choice.'
○ To get more hands up in response to a question: 'Come on, only three people can answer this? Surely not? Come on, let's have some more!'
○ To quieten a class: 'I'm asking you politely.'
○ To get the general noise level down: 'I would like the noise level down please. Five, four, three, two, one!'

MAGIC PHRASES

Picture the following situation: a child has played up in your lesson so badly that despite all warnings he has to be moved to a discipline support room. He refuses to go and becomes abusive and threatening saying 'Why should I move, he's been saying stuff about my mum! It's him that should be moved!' He starts to throw stuff around, swear and this, of course, wrecks your attempts to teach.

How do you feel?

I know that many teachers at this point feel like chucking in teaching altogether. They reason that it's hard enough with all the workload to cope with extreme behaviour on top. I know for a fact that many a good teacher has thrown in the towel for this very reason.

I have found that looking at the situation in a different way has helped me cope with this challenging but rewarding job. First of all remember that the situation outlined above and indeed any extreme behaviour is comparatively rare. However, when it does happen you have to deal with it. If you don't, or can't, who will?

When confronted with this sort of behaviour always stay calm. In addition say to yourself 'This is a very difficult situation to deal with. It is rare but I will need to concentrate and handle this carefully and skilfully.' Don't be frightened of it.

Whatever technique you use, and whatever the difficult situation, do take time to reflect on it afterwards. Discuss it with colleagues and ask for their advice and opinion. Listen and learn from their stories of difficult situations. You will automatically realize then that there is really nothing wrong with you.

The nature of teaching does involve some really awful situations. If you deploy the strategies and the philosophy of common sense expounded in this book you will hopefully reduce the likelihood of really difficult situations developing in the first place. But they do happen. When they do, approach them with the right mental attitude and instead of chucking in the towel you will learn from them and become an even better, stronger and more effective teacher. The point is, adopt the right way of looking at it and it will help you cope.

Keeping things on track in the classroom

IDEA 25

TALK UP THE CLASS

At the start of the lesson recount the good points of the last lesson. I find that mentioning specific instances of improvement as students come through the door really acts as a boost to their confidence. For example, you could congratulate:

o Dewi for arriving on time to lessons;
o Matthew for staying in his seat more;
o Helen for an overall improvement in presentation.

Emphasize how happy you are with their progress. By doing this on a regular basis, you talk the class up and create a good relationship with them. It also gives the message that you're always looking out for improvements, however slight.

It can be difficult to start a lesson. Often the whole group seems completely uninterested in anything. So, how do you awaken their desire to get started? A great way to do this is to remind the class of the really good things they did in the last lesson. In particular, pick out the names of students who did well (try not to always pick the same people!) and encourage them to do even better in the current lesson. For example:

- ○ 'Meera – well done on completing the written task last lesson. I'm sure you'll do well at today's task.'
- ○ 'Jack – you managed to understand "x" concept last lesson. Let's see how well we can build on that this lesson.'

The great thing about this technique is that it anticipates a good lesson. Many teachers start off with a moan, and I've even seen teachers writing names on the board for detention at the beginning of the lesson – this is a big mistake!

With this method you quickly set up a strong sense of success and because it's based on the last lesson it makes everyone feel confident that they can achieve at least as well as last time.

Of course, to get the best from this you must remember to keep good outline notes of what happened in each lesson and highlight which students did particularly well.

Once you have delivered this upbeat message you can launch straight into your starter.

IDEA 27

A great way to involve students right at the start of the lesson, and therefore minimize opportunities for poor behaviour, is to have a set of flash cards ready with answers to simple questions with one-word answers written on them. For example, 'What is the capital of France?' It's good to use A4 cards with large lettering and it works well if the cards are in a variety of different, bright colours.

Hand the cards to students as they come in and then start asking them questions. To reply they must hold up the correct card. For example, the student who has Paris would hold up their card in response to the question mentioned above. You can of course adapt the questions for any subject. It has the advantage of:

○ involving the students straight away in the lesson and focusing their attention on you;
○ giving them something physical to do;
○ being easy for them as no writing is required;
○ allowing them to respond without talking.

IDEA

28

Although it seems straightforward, handing out materials can cause chaos. To minimize disruption have a carefully worked out system in place.

Don't give out work yourself as it's when your back is turned that problems emerge. Instead, have a rota of monitors recorded on your seating plan. With monitors you can stand at the front and command the situation – it's a bit like directing the traffic!

○ Make sure that your monitors have a particular row or group which they work to.
○ Always insist that the students put their pens down and listen carefully before work is collected in.
○ Make sure that you allow plenty of time to do this to avoid rush and chaos when the bell goes.

Explain exactly how you want the work before it's collected in. For example:

> *'Please close your exercise books and put the blue sheet next to it. Take the green sheet home for homework. Now monitors, please listen carefully. Collect in a neat pile the exercise books from your row and a set of blue sheets. Right, collect them in now please.'*

If you stick to this system of rota and monitors the students will get used to it and it will save you a lot of time and trouble.

GIVING AND COLLECTING WORK

33

THE MAGIC THREE

Rather than making the whole class do the same task, try giving them a choice of three tasks. These can be clearly set out on the white board. Give the class time to decide and then ask them to write their choice in their books. Now as they start their tasks you can go around the class to check what they've chosen.

I find that there's something about giving this choice of tasks which makes the work more attractive to the students (they like the feeling of autonomy). But beware, if you have more than three choices it can sometimes lead to a 'spoilt for choice' situation whereupon no task is actually chosen.

To help the logistics of this idea I find that three piles of colour-coded worksheets helps to start the students working. For example, on the board it will indicate: 1 = blue sheet; 2 = orange; 3 = green.

Sometimes it's difficult to get students to start working. One of the main reasons for this is that students become negative if they feel the work is either too easy or too difficult for them. This initial refusal to start can quickly spread around the class and can be very dispiriting for the teacher.

Start off with a multiple-choice sheet (which can be adapted to fit any subject area). This sheet should contain questions with at least three possible answers. Having a firm written task automatically settles the class. What's more, as the work is pitched at the right level it allows them to have a go straight away. Once they're settled into this you can then introduce more challenging work.

THE BEAUTY OF CHOICE

BROADCASTING THE POSITIVE

There is a crucial phase in a lesson, just where you want the work to begin, where obstacles can stop the lesson it in its tracks. The worst-case scenario is when you have set things up for the pupils to start their work when a loud mouth pushes the work away and says 'I'm not doing this!' and because the loud mouth is influential in the group others follow. It is an alarming situation for a teacher when many in the group refuse to work. You feel, with despair, that the balance of power has shifted.

A good thing to do at this point is to walk around in an encouraging way and as you circulate around the class make your presence felt, listen out and look out for positive things connected to the early progress of work which they are doing. You can then broadcast this back to the class. For example: 'Good, Sara's starting a great map, I heard Peter discussing the chart with David just then, now I want to go back to Gemma to see how she's progressing with that table of facts. You want some coloured pencils for your picture, OK Jo I shall get those as soon as I've seen Gemma!'

Notice an important thing. You don't necessarily have to say good things. Just reporting back what they are doing will do. The point is that you are telling the rest of the class that most of the class are progressing.

This has a profound effect on the class. It is no longer you trying to urge them to work or telling them off for not working. These obstacles to work are melted away because you are highlighting and emphasizing the progress already being made and you are feeding back to the whole class.

The group as a whole takes on a momentum at this point with the sense that the whole class is moving forward and the inertia of this energy carries on and takes the focus off of you as leader. It automatically reduces confrontation. It is like a boat which is under way and the comments you broadcast about this and that going well, giving names and specific things happening, become like the oars in the water propelling the class along.

So to extend the analogy, adopt the role of coxswain, keep an eye on everything and keep broadcasting the good stuff as your class glides swiftly forward.

If some of your students are having problems getting started with a specific task, giving them an extra help sheet is a good idea. This sheet should break down the task into smaller chunks and, if necessary, contain a sample answer for them to copy to get them started.

It is well worth spending a fair bit of time designing 'user friendly' help sheets as they can be used as an effective support to normal teaching materials. Explain to the student that as they're having trouble starting you have prepared a special 'booster' for them. But don't give them out too easily, or everyone will want one!

This frees you up to circulate around the class and help others. When used carefully the extra help sheet is like having an additional assistant in the room with you.

EXTRA HELP FOR YOU AND THEM

Newspapers make a bland story appear interesting by their use of 'getting an angle' on a story. Likewise you can enhance the interest value and impact of a piece of information by giving it 'an angle'.

Here are some examples from different subject areas:

To teach a football technique you might begin by saying: 'Did you see Wayne Rooney the other day? The particular technique he used is easier to learn than you think.'

To teach about a certain method in art you may introduce it with: 'I wonder if anyone here saw Rolf Harris when he painted the Queen. He used this method . . .'

To teach about angles in mathematics you could show an OHT of the mathematical bridge at Cambridge and ask: 'Can any one guess what is unusual about this bridge?' This then provides a lead into your explaining about angles.

To teach about microwaves in science you might start by holding up an egg and asking: 'If I put this egg into a microwave oven and turned it on, what do you think would happen?'

The great thing about this is that it warms up the interest of the students and makes it easier to hold their attention when you start to explain something.

The above are just a few examples to show the sort of thing that can be done and with a little bit of research, preparation and imagination you can find hundreds of ways to bring the start of your lesson to life in this way.

USING AN AUDIO TAPE

Record an audio tape of a reading of a piece of text. Try to make it about five minutes long and either record your own voice or, even better, that of a colleague. Prepare a copy of the text as a handout and give this to the class. Play the tape asking the students to follow it on their handout.

The change of hearing a recorded voice, instead of you speaking, really interests students. This also allows you to keep your eyes on the class and make non-verbal signs to keep them listening, rather than concentrating on reading yourself.

If you refer to a visual, at that point in the tape you can hold it up to show the class, which also heightens their interest.

Students also love to hear music. If you can find a piece that's relevant to the lesson, play it to conclude. You will find this lesson really sticks in your students' minds.

A market pitcher makes his living by attracting a crowd of people to his stall, interesting them in the product and then selling it to them.

It is useful to note the similarity between the market pitcher and the teacher. Although you don't have to attract a crowd, you do have to engage interest and then sell students a learning activity.

I have found that some of the techniques of the market pitchers can be adapted with tremendous results in the classroom. For example, instead of going through the same thing in the same way with a monotone voice saying: 'Come on, pay attention, turn to page 14 and carry on' sort of routine, why not 'set your stall'? Have a selection of tasks students could do and have these ready displayed on the board.

Try engaging interest by adapting a sort of banter to draw them in. For example: 'Come on everyone, you all look tired today, what's wrong with you? Come on, have a look at this. Now, I've got three activities for you to choose from to get you started today. Look, there's the pink one if you fancy a bit of drawing to get you going. I've seen some great little drawings done from this one. Those ones are in that tray, but don't touch them yet. Are you paying attention at the back? Come on, it's taken me a long time to get all this ready, so you'll enjoy it more. Come on, now listen.' You then point to the blue one amplifying your body language to direct their attention to the board. Practise the rhythm of your talk and the rhythm of your body language. You will straight away notice an increase in their attention levels as they respond to this type of presentation.

You may wish to continue along these lines: 'Rather than the pink one you may wish to start with the

TRY PITCHING YOUR WARES

blue one. Look, there're some words to match up with meanings. They're really very unusual words, the other group loved that one. It's all set out on the sheet, look. Which one would you prefer to start with? Or if you don't fancy either of those what about this green one? Now this is a good one. You have to do a few easy sums on this one. If you're quite good at numbers this is the one for you. Just to get you started. Come on, make your minds up. Which one do you want?'

It helps if you have the sheets colour-coded and set out neatly in trays for ease of distribution. Whatever the subject you can adapt a variety of types of thinking skills to get them started. The technique of begging the question, asking if they prefer this one or that one helps them to 'buy' the learning activity.

You will find that the lively banter is appreciated by the students as they see you trying to make the lesson more interesting. It overcomes the negative reactions which you often initially get from some groups of unmotivated students. The great thing is that this gets the lesson off the ground and makes it easier when you introduce the next task for them to do.

It is very tempting to carry a lesson directly on from the last one. However, you might find some problems arising from this. Materials you wanted your students to bring just don't appear. Or students may be at various stages of completion, so it can be difficult to restart the lesson and keep up the momentum.

If, however, you start a new and different lesson each time you can lose the sense of continuity. So aim to make your lessons completely self-contained to get your students starting on the work together. This work should, however, link with your previous lesson. As the lesson progresses you can bring in further links from the last lesson where appropriate. This gets over the problem of those who missed the previous lesson and it allows keen students to revisit their work to finish it off or expand it. The beauty of this is that you achieve the best of both worlds: continuity and an organized restart.

THE 'SELF-CONTAINED' LESSON

BRIDGING ACTIVITIES

Changing activities within a lesson can often cause problems. Some students will want to carry on with what they're doing and the teacher will be strongly tempted to just let the activity drift on as it's easier that way.

However, a good way to change activities is to use a 'buffer' or a 'bridge' activity. It will round off the last piece of work, raise interest levels and kick start the new section of the lesson.

Ask for a volunteer to come to the front and tell the class three key things about the area of study you have just been working on. I find there's always one who will come up to do this. The fact that someone new (other than you) is at the front seems to grab the class's attention. If the student gets stuck, either ask for one other student to come up and help out, or offer to help yourself. Use this to conclude the work just done and then present the next activity.

It is essential to learn techniques that provide smooth transition from one activity to another. Following on from Idea 37, here are some more tips.

Students will get used to a clear signal and a clear routine. For example, ask them to stop writing and then wait, repeating the request if necessary, until they have. Now you can give your instructions. Remember to keep them clear, short and to the point. Have a visual back-up which you can point to. Repeat your instructions clearly, then have a 'trigger' phrase like: 'OK let's move on to the new activity now. Stop the old one or we'll run out of time!'

You will find that as long as the materials they need are well organized and your visual back-up is prominent, together with a strong clear routine, then the students will get used to changing activities smoothly. It will raise efficiency and reduce stress.

HOW TO CHANGE ACTIVITIES

Teachers tend to stand and talk to the class as a matter of habit. Part of the art of teaching involves attracting and holding the attention of the class through a variety of techniques. A really effective one is to hold up a large envelope and show it to the class. On it are large letters saying 'IMPORTANT'. You make quite a show of opening it as you say: 'Mr Smith has asked me to read this important announcement to you'. Note that it is wise to choose a teacher who is in authority and who you know the students respect. Check with the teacher beforehand and you will find they are always pleased to agree to go along with this one. The beauty of the note is that you can gear it to anything which is an issue to you. For example, supposing there was far too much chewing of gum last lesson and they weren't responding to your requests to stop. The next lesson you say to the class: 'I have spent a lot of time discussing the problem we had last lesson concerning the chewing of gum with Mr Smith. Do you remember, when I asked you to stop and a lot of you wouldn't? Well listen to this': then read them the announcement (which you typed the night before) keeping it short. An example would be:

> *Mr Young has explained to me the problems last lesson with the chewing of gum. I have asked Mr Young to give me the names of all students who continue to ignore this school rule. [signed Mr Smith]*

Then you carry on with your lesson exactly as normal.

The advantages of this idea are:

○ You can adapt it to any problem which is bothering you with their behaviour.

- It shows the students that you do not forget problems from last lesson, but you follow them up efficiently.
- The students are shown that it is not just you alone trying to reinforce the rules, but the whole system.
- It is a powerful way to back up what you say with minimal bother to the senior staff.
- There is something about the written word which seems to carry more authority than the spoken word.

IDEA 40

THE BRILLIANT 'BREAK'

Sometimes it's a good idea to give your class a break. If given now and again, and timed well, it's brilliant. Don't overdo it though, as they'll come to expect it every lesson.

If the students have done well, tell them so and give them three minutes to chat quietly while preparing for the next task. Once the time is up have a strong signal to let them know the next task is beginning. The students will appreciate that you're trying to help them and they'll cooperate. Make two important conditions for the break:

1 Noise must be kept to a reasonable level.
2 The students must pay attention when the new task starts.

Have a moment in your lesson known as: 'The quiet thought for the day'. To signal this have two supporting devices:

1 A nicely produced sign mounted on stiff card which is colourful and bold with the words: 'The quiet thought for the day' and a symbol. The sign should be A3 size.
2 A short (ten-second) signature tune. A short sequence from distinctive classical music works well. Have this ready on an audio tape player.

You can include your thought for the day at any time during the lesson depending on your own judgement as to where it will fit in best.

When the time is right you announce: 'Time for the quiet thought for the day' in an upbeat enthusiastic voice and then hold up the sign and play the 'signature tune'. When done on a regular basis it is surprising how well the students react to this. It will become a positive habit.

When you first start doing it keep it short, punchy and crisp. As they get more used to it you can develop and lengthen it. The topic can be anything which gives food for thought. It can be linked to the subject or to wider issues. You always support it with the reassuring voice that education should not be trapped into narrow subject areas only but should be about thinking about life itself. You can pick up on ideas raised in assemblies or at tutor time.

The great thing about this is when the routine for doing it is well established it calms the class and the sign and music trigger powerful expectation and compliance. You will find that it is a useful addition to your armoury for having a well-ordered, settled class and is a great way to get information

THE QUIET THOUGHT FOR THE DAY

across as they get used to listening out for this highlight of the lesson.

Here are a few examples of the quiet thought for the day you could have. Keep your own book of them and add to them:

SLOW DOWN

We tend to rush from the moment we get up in the morning. Rush, rush, rush. We rush

- our breakfast
- getting dressed
- to school
- to break
- home
- and then out

The quiet thought for the day is 'Slow down!' Enjoy the moment. Look at things carefully. Concentrate on one thing, like a tree or a little bird drinking in a puddle. Think how beautiful it is. Say to yourself 'Stop rushing, slow down and enjoy this moment.'

Another thing, students. If you do this regularly, you will enjoy life more. Perhaps tomorrow one of you can tell me if you managed to stop and enjoy the moment.

FREEDOM

We all want freedom. Some of you feel restricted by school. You have to be here, but you'd rather be somewhere else. It seems like, in the future, when you leave school, you can do whatever you want and have all the freedom in the world. But it isn't as simple as that. Millions of people work at jobs which restrict their freedom in order to get money to allow them to have a home and eat. You will find in life that you give up some freedoms in order to get others. Why not make the most of your school days? You have to be here anyway. Think about the day you leave. Do you want to look back at endless arguments and rebellion with very little to show for it? Or do you want to look back at your best efforts making the most of things? Just think, you could end up with lots of knowledge and skills to show for it. That day will come. How do you want it to be for you?

IDEA
42

A common problem for teachers is the speed at which they operate. It is natural with 30 people demanding your attention to respond quickly to get everyone's problems sorted. Remember that the demand on your time in the lesson will always vastly outstrip your ability to sort everything out. If you go too fast, two negative things will happen.

1 You will burn yourself out.
2 The quality of your teaching is reduced because of the speed at which it's delivered.

To try and avoid this:

o make it a habit to ask yourself, from time to time, whether you're going too fast;
o do things one at a time and at a steady pace;
o refuse to be interrupted when you are giving individual help;
o remind the students that you're trying to help everyone but you can only do one thing at a time.

You will find that you'll be left with more energy and your students will actually learn more from you.

A good way of reinforcing a particular message about behaviour in the classroom is to have well-presented posters around your walls. These confirm what you're saying when you remind a student of an important ground rule. If, for example, a student keeps calling out, remind them of the 'hands up rule' and then point to a poster which refers to it. This has a far greater impact and effectively gets your point across.

IDEA

43

VISUAL REINFORCEMENT

I observed a lesson once where a teacher, who was very popular with the students, was in full swing. She was giving out information, pointing to things on the flip chart, sticking up OHTs and making good use of the PowerPoint with wonderful graphics. At times she held up an object in the air, put on a funny hat to make a point about something and at one stage even danced, to the delight of the students. She would occasionally ask a student a question and in reply to his one-word answer would punch the air and sing 'Great!'

It was clear that the students were well behaved and that the teacher was popular. Despite all this I was left, after the lesson, with a sense of unease and it got me wondering.

As a passive observer it was easy for me to put myself in the shoes of the students. I was seeing this teacher putting on a great show, but if I had been a student I would have soon figured out that the chance of me actually being asked a question was quite small. All I really had to do was sit still and watch. In fact I could easily drift off and daydream and even if my name was called I could just shake myself and meekly say 'Sorry, I missed that one, could you say it again?'

At the end of the lesson the teacher looked completely exhausted. I'm sure that the teacher had the sense of having done her best and delivered an excellent lesson. My feelings of unease about the whole thing were to do with how little the students had actually done, and how difficult it was to know how much they had learnt.

The point here is that the teacher was doing all the work. You want to aim for a lesson where the bulk of the work is done by the students themselves. Good behaviour of students is what this book is all about, but we have to be clear about this point. Good behaviour should be a route to good learning. Yes, of course your role is to show, demonstrate, explain and teach but there must be a point when it is their turn to work on something. Once this happens you can turn your role into that of supervisor and can encourage individuals to stay on task.

If you don't get this balance of strategic use of energy right you will exhaust yourself and not be able to keep going in the long run. In return the students will do very little themselves and as a result their learning will suffer.

BEHAVIOUR TRACKING CHARTS

For this system to work it must be kept simple and followed up in every lesson.

Towards the end of the lesson allocate a behaviour code to each student. This can be done in a positive and upbeat way. I find four categories work well. For example:

o dark green = room for improvement;
o blue = satisfactory;
o orange = good;
o yellow = excellent.

Sum up quickly towards the end of the lesson (reminders during the lesson) and say things like:

o 'Darren, you have definitely improved with your behaviour today, you get Orange.'
o 'Wayne, I must say I'm a bit disappointed and you know why. I've got to give you Dark Green.'

Follow up by having a large chart on the wall with the students' names clearly displayed down the left-hand side. Each lesson colour in the boxes so that everyone's behaviour and progress is there for all to see. You will be pleasantly surprised to find that the students will want to earn a good behaviour colour and that they'll compete with each other. Keep this simple and straightforward, attend to it every lesson and draw attention to it regularly. Explain that copies go to the head of subject and are used at parents' evenings. Indeed, individual records can easily be sent home each half-term.

A good idea for keeping up the self-esteem of students over a long period of time is to use 'Best work and achievement folders'. Clearly label each folder with the name of each student and keep them in the classroom at all times.

Encourage students to put particularly good pieces of work into their folder. If something good happens to them, or they are proud of something, encourage them to make a note of it and pop it in the folder. You may find that it takes a fair bit of persistence on your part to get this system up and running, but with patience it will more than repay your initial efforts.

When the student has low self-esteem or motivation sit down for a few moments with them and go through the folder. It does have an uplifting effect. Over time the students will be pleasantly surprised at how much is in there.

Be active in looking out for things that the student could include. In conversation with the student if you hear of something good, why not make a brief note and pop it in the folder? It gives a strong message to the student that you're encouraging them to do well.

BEST WORK AND ACHIEVEMENT FOLDERS

IDEA

47

MANAGING A DISCUSSION

Managing a discussion can sometimes seem impossible, especially when students all call out at the same time and don't listen to one another.

An easy and effective method to manage a discussion is to arrange the class into four teams, each with a nominated captain. Write on the board the names of the team captains with room for recording any points scored or deducted. The captain must choose who speaks from their team (obviously make sure that this is fair). The teams get a point if they contribute a constructive comment to the discussion. And each time someone calls out without permission, a point is deducted from their team score. The competitive element keeps the classroom on track.

Insist that the students put their hands up when they wish to ask questions or contribute to discussions.

A common problem is that a student puts up his or her hand and then speaks anyway. So, it's a good idea to designate times in the lesson when you're quite clear that you don't want anybody to put their hand up as everybody should be listening. If somebody puts their hand up during that time, stop and remind them of your rule. You will find that if you stick rigidly to this the students will get used to, and comply with, your system.

To reinforce this, make it a habit to congratulate students who stick to the protocol. Continue to reprimand those who break the rule and praise those who keep to it and you will gradually win the class round.

IDEA

48

THE HANDS UP REMINDER

TIME FOR INSTRUCTIONS

When you give instructions or ask questions of the students, build in a period of time for them to take in what you've said or asked. Become an expert on the timing of this. Don't always pick the first hand that goes up. Give the students thinking time and encourage more to put their hands up.

This issue of timing is crucial in getting the best from your students.

If you ask a question you often find that the usual 'few' will put up their hands and the usual 'many' will not. Often the ones who put up their hands can use their body language and voice to command attention. They are used to repeating this pattern in every lesson. So, it's a good idea to alternate the way in which you ask your class questions.

For example, give the students a spare piece of paper each. Ask a question and allow a few moments for them to jot down an answer on the paper. Encourage them to have a go even if they're not sure. Then you can ask them what they've written on the paper, or walk round the room and just look at the answers. This is a useful alternative to the hands up approach and involves more of the students without embarrassing them.

QUESTIONING THE CLASS

DEALING WITH THE WRONG ANSWER

If you ask your class a question, there will always be some students who answer incorrectly. The challenge is how to react to this. For example, if you say 'Good' to encourage them, then you can cause confusion because the answer is wrong. If you say 'No, that's not the right answer,' you could dampen their confidence and they may not contribute any more. It is important to create an atmosphere where the wrong answer is welcome.

The key is to make sure all the students participate. You could say something like: 'I see what it is you're thinking. Well done for trying. That's not the correct answer this time. Try again in a minute though, won't you?' Give them an encouraging smile and move on.

You could use instances of when famous people got it wrong, for example: 'Edison produced hundreds of "wrong" light bulbs before he achieved success.'

Continuing the theme of Idea 50, questions can be tailored to make them a fair and useful experience for everyone. Below is an example of questioning that I've used to great effect to get whole-class participation.

Give out coloured cards, apparently at random, to all members of the class. Tell them that their cards are for them to jot down answers and that you've also put some clues on the back. You now have groups of students each with the same colour. But beforehand you've decided which student will have which colour card. With the help of your seating plan and the way the cards are sorted you can quickly give them out to the right students.

The idea is this – you've worked out the ability of each student and the clues on the back of the cards are tailored to support their particular ability range. For example, the clue on one colour card may say: 'Question 1: The capital of France is Par_ _' for the less able. For the more able, maybe: 'The capital of France is _ _ _ _ _? (Clue: it has the Eiffel Tower)', and so on.

Now when you ask questions you can turn it into a fun game, for example: 'Question 1, what is the capital of France? Only the yellow cards may answer this one. If you get stuck look on the back of the card for clues.'

This way you can control who answers and you can support each student's answer without actually saying anything. The system ensures that everyone can join in.

USING THE BEST IDEAS FROM OTHER SUBJECTS

A great strategy for dealing with challenging behaviour is to exchange the techniques that work well in other subject areas. Teachers tend to get trapped within their own department and short-sightedness can creep in. A wider perspective can be very helpful.

In practical terms arrange a meeting, say every couple of months, with teachers from other subject areas and find out what special strategies for behaviour control they employ. A lot of these can be easily adapted for use in your subject area. It's even better to observe other lessons to see how an idea works.

Ideas that I've seen work to great effect are listed below.

o In physical education a five minute physical warm-up session is used. Why not use that in your subject, to kick start the brain?

o In technology the teacher may have a cabinet with marked places for all the tools to go back to before anyone can be dismissed. A similar idea could be employed to get the equipment back in other subjects to save end of lesson searches and arguments. Any help with organization efficiency automatically helps with managing behaviour.

o In drama the command 'freeze' is often used. This could be very useful!

The more ideas you have the better, and the great thing is that other teachers have already tried and tested their ideas for you and the students are used to going along with them.

Many teachers have had the horrific experience of a physical fight between two students in their classroom. When analysing what happened you almost always find that if the teacher had intervened earlier he or she could have stopped the fight before it started.

It's a good idea to develop a 'nose' for a particular type of behaviour between students which signals there's trouble ahead, and you must always be on the lookout for it. Adopt a no-nonsense approach. If, for example, they ignore your requests to stop the name calling then you ask one of them to step outside the room and call for assistance.

With practice you will identify the type of banter which is normal for a particular group, and aggressive behaviour which, if left unchecked, could easily escalate into a fight. It is quite rare but when it happens it must be dealt with by early, brisk and firm intervention.

PREVENTING FIGHTS

AFTER A BAD LESSON

Sometimes a lesson will go so badly that the teacher feels he or she has completely lost control and will dread seeing that class again.

Try and deal with a really bad lesson in a systematic and logical way. The worst thing to do is to carry on the next lesson as if nothing has happened. If you do that the same problems will be back to haunt you.

Try asking for help. Run through what you attempted to do and how it all went wrong with your head of department or a senior teacher. Action should be seen to be taken the very next lesson. So, start the next lesson with a senior teacher in the room and with the ringleaders isolated in a discipline support supervision room. If possible, arrange for that teacher to stay the whole lesson. If that can't be arranged then try to get somebody to help you at the start and end of the lesson. Having another teacher there shows the students that they're not just taking you on but the whole teaching network.

The next lesson with the class who seriously played you up is very important. The objective of this lesson is for you to regain full control of the situation and the class. At the start explain briefly what went wrong. For example:

'Obviously last lesson wasn't good. A lot of students ignored my instructions. Some of the main students who did are not with this group today because of that. I want good behaviour today so that we can all carry on learning. That is why we are here.'

Make sure that the work for this lesson is very clear and straightforward. Remember, the chief objective is to regain control. You will find the lesson will go well but don't become complacent. You still have to reintegrate the ringleaders back into your group (see Idea 56).

This idea follows on from Idea 55, where troublesome ringleaders have been isolated from the class. The best way to reintegrate them is with senior management support. You can try bringing them back one by one over a series of lessons, or maybe two at a time. The important thing is to show the student that their previous behaviour was totally unacceptable. It crossed your 'bottom line'.

You can then continue with your lessons using all the techniques and ideas outlined in this book. A particular focus could be to perhaps let little things go so as to not aggravate the situation. You will find that by using this method the lesson will return to a manageable level. If you still encounter serious recurrent problems with the same students, there may be a strong case for an exchange with other groups.

REINTEGRATING RINGLEADERS

TACKLING TESTS

In teaching you need to test your students in order to see how much they've learnt. But the problem is there are just too many tests and naturally students get fed up with them. The word 'test' sets up the wrong associations, so try calling them something different. Phrases that have worked well for me are:

o fun 'feedback' sessions;
o 'how much can you remember?' sessions;
o 'impress me with your knowledge in just ten minutes' sessions.

Use your imagination to present tests in a positive light and you'll find students are much more willing.

Setting and collecting in homework for a challenging group can become a nightmare.

Set a piece of written homework with at least a week or more in which to do it. This gives you time to collect it in and then remind the stragglers when it's due. Make a big deal of that one written piece. Another reminder can be given at the next lesson. Spare instructions can be on hand.

If homework is still missing keep back the culprits. Explain that you've reminded them three times and if it's not in next lesson a lunchtime detention will be set. Follow through with the lunchtime detention as a last resort.

Only when that piece of homework is fully sorted out for all students in the class do you progress to the next piece of homework. This gives the strong signal that homework is important, that they have plenty of time and reminders and that you won't give up. You are also allowing yourself more time for chase ups and organization.

MAKING HOMEWORK MORE MANAGEABLE

SETTING FUN HOMEWORK

Be creative when setting homework. Ask your students to do something related to their own interests and to give some quick oral feedback in the next lesson. For example, ask them to prepare a quick summary of their favourite hobby or pastime. You can alternate this type of homework with the more formal written request.

By being creative, the students will enjoy it more and it will therefore be easier to manage.

Marking books can be a time-consuming activity. With students with challenging behaviour the sad truth is that they often don't even read the comments you have spent hours writing. So, a good idea is to develop a quick-fire system that is rapid enough for you to mark the entire set of books after each lesson. It won't take you long but it really benefits the students.

Have separate scales for effort, output and quality and give them marks out of ten for each of these. You could also have a chart on the wall on which you display the results lesson by lesson. (You can have a more thorough and detailed mark on a periodic basis, for example once a fortnight.) The beauty of the quick-fire system is that you can give feedback quickly and efficiently at the start of the lesson about how they did in the last lesson. There are lots of advantages with this quick-fire system, for example:

○ there's a built-in target-setting process which is simple and effective;
○ students have fast feedback;
○ students know each lesson that you're going to definitely look at their work and this makes them work better;
○ simplified responses are easy to understand.

The key point is to keep the system simple to use so you can maintain a consistent approach across each term.

MARKING

CONTROLLING THE END OF A LESSON

Although the below takes a bit of organizing it will pay back huge dividends in the next lesson and throughout the term. Write down on a large sheet of paper two clear points about the next lesson under the headings:

1 This is what we are going to do next lesson.
2 This is why we are going to do it.

Remember to keep it clear and simple. Then ask the students to think about how you are going to tackle the task. A huge advantage is the consistency this gives at the start of the next lesson. Show them the sheet with the outline and repeat it. You will find that if you make a habit of this (which doesn't take long) it registers that you are organized and that there is a clear structure to the work. It sends strong signals to your students that you know exactly what you're doing.

SECTION

4

Dealing with
common problems

GETTING TO THE ROOT OF A PROBLEM

Very often a significant proportion of disruption in a classroom is of a recurrent type. It is not all that easy to spot, particularly when the teacher is in full stride of classroom activities. In practice what happens is that the teacher reprimands the student each time something goes wrong, but unfortunately the root cause of the problem remains.

A good way to tackle this one is to try to identify where these problems are and take a bit of time to investigate what is going on.

For example, if a student is regularly late, is there a pattern to this? Perhaps it is always the afternoon lesson and maybe it is because he goes home for lunch. Are a certain group of students often late after PE? Perhaps they are not getting enough time to change out of their PE kit. After break do certain students disrupt the class because they have been playing football, forgot to get a drink and arrive thirsty to your lesson ?

The key thing here is to keep good, clear, accurate notes to help you identify 'hot spot' areas. Share your information with other teachers to help establish patterns.

The next step is to approach the student with the attitude that you want to find out what is causing the problem and help them solve it. Don't be confrontational.

I have known serious and recurrent disruption problems, which have gone on for weeks, be sorted out after some probing and the removal of the cause. The problem is that often teachers do not have time to step back and identify that there is a pattern to the problem.

Getting to the root of a 'pattern' problem can take time but it does have distinct advantages:

○ Once the cause of a problem has been found, it can be removed and lots of continued reprimands become unnecessary.

○ Students perceive that you are trying to help them rather than always telling them off and they go along with this attitude.

○ You gain valuable information from other teachers which helps you even further in the overall picture.

○ The students pick up that you are a professional who is prepared to take time and patience to get to the heart of tricky problems.

It is very frustrating for a teacher to be faced with a request to help a student who clearly needs it, and yet not be able to do so because the noise levels and disruption of the class increase as soon as the students know that they're not being watched.

So how do you manage this situation? A good idea is to call the student up to your desk, get him or her to stand to one side so that you can look at his or her work and discuss it while still watching the class. As you look at the work keep commenting on individuals in the class. This works well because the class will hear these comments and know that everyone is under your watchful gaze!

In the case of a low-ability group it is frequently the case that, when tests, assessments or mock exams are done, the results are very low. The students, whose self-esteem can often already be low, will consider the low grades as proof that they are going to fail. They wonder what is the point of further study, and the lack of interest and subsequent poor behaviour that they have already shown may get even worse. The teacher's power to manage behaviour is weakened by this situation.

So what does a teacher do? Not to disclose the grades can make the situation worse. A good way is to be very careful and thoughtful with the way you explain or 're-frame' the situation. You

○ explain that the grades show what they are capable of now and that the harder they work between now and the exams the better their grades will be
○ focus on the future and say that employers would prefer them to have some sort of grade rather than nothing at all
○ remind them that getting no results at all indicates a complete lack of interest
○ tell them that the right positive attitude and effort can restart here today and who knows where it will lead

Your trump card is to explain that the reference from the school as to how well they behave and how hard they try is a crucial thing. Give them examples of past students who on paper perhaps didn't look too great academically but with their right attitude and efforts applied themselves to a particular profession and became successful in it.

This sort of positive pep talk presented in a sincere way really does help keep the students on track. Coupled with your individual knowledge of each student's hopes and plans it will help you win through with them despite the worst grades.

Keep a log of past students who have done well in their jobs despite poor grades and use those, of course with their prior permission, as examples to inspire your present students.

As icing on the cake hold up your book of past successes and ask: 'Come on, who in this room am I going to be able to add to this book next year?' Give a dramatic pause for it to sink in and then get on with the lesson.

There is one more step. In some cases, if you can keep in touch with previous students and make them 'friends of the school', it is a massive boost to invite them back in to talk about how they have done. I have found this to be extremely encouraging to students of low ability.

It is a great idea to build up a good network of contacts at your school so that you can arrange for other teachers to pop in and support you, even if it's only for a few minutes at the beginning and end of lessons.

You can arrange to return the favour in your free periods. This is a great investment.

GETTING SUPPORT

THE STRATEGIC BLIND EYE

One of the tensions with challenging behaviour is maintaining a balance between getting the lesson flowing and not allowing unruly students to behave exactly as they like.

It is easy to get into confrontational situations and get involved in energy sapping rows (your energy, not theirs). On top of this, other students are ready to pounce if they see anything other than fair play!

Think of your lesson as a carriage on a journey. Make sure you fit your wheels with 'springs' to absorb the annoying little things. Without the springs you can find yourself reacting to every jolt along the way. A lot of those little jolts can be tactically ignored. (I've touched on this briefly in Idea 56.) However, be strategic in your approach – if something is important then you should deal with it. This approach saves you energy and keeps the lesson flowing better. In a nutshell, see everything that is going on but only react to selected things.

Sometimes a group arrives to your class and for one reason or another they will not settle down and stop talking because of something that has just happened. It could be, for example, that they were caught up watching a fight just before the lesson.

Here is an idea to counter this situation which will work well if used with discretion.

If you feel that you really cannot quench the heat of the chatter tell them that you really must get on with the lesson and announce this sentence: 'I'll tell you what I'm prepared to do as a compromise. You obviously are ignoring me because something exceptional has happened. I don't want to know what has happened but you may speak about it for four minutes on condition that when you hear the signal you start work without further delay!'

You then allow them the four minutes to get it 'out of their system'. As they are talking you give very powerful body language which strongly suggests that you are preparing everything for the start. For example, you may wish to write a few things on the board and check your watch a few times.

When the time comes to give the signal announce it clearly. (The signal could be a bell or a clap or a sharp bang on the desk – whatever works best for you.) You then get on with the lesson.

If you get further disruption calmly say: 'Come on, now, I've kept to my side of the bargain, now you keep to yours!' Be bold and matter of fact and then get on quickly with your lesson.

You will find that this works well because most students have a sense of fair play and they feel that they have negotiated a 'bargain'. To prevent repetitions, make sure that you make it clear that this is an exceptional matter.

IRRESISTIBLE CHAT

Some students appear friendly, polite and cooperative but do not complete any work. They may well make token efforts but they're really not working at all. There is a huge temptation with a challenging group to let these students get away with it. After all, they're not holding you up from teaching the rest. You must, however, make sure that you tackle this one. If you don't two serious problems will occur. First, the student will be entrenched in the habit of doing no work, and if this is allowed it will become virtually impossible to get him or her to work and s/he therefore won't learn much. Second, many of the students will have a great excuse not to work, citing him or her as an example.

Therefore, keep chipping away and monitor how much he or she is doing by setting step-by-step targets. Explain that he or she is a very pleasant student but that he or she is there is to learn. In most cases, when students realize you won't give up they start to work.

If you see that students are repeatedly making unkind comments to another student then you must give warnings for the behaviour to stop and a report must be sent to the head of year straight away.

If the comments continue, remove all of the students who ignore your instructions to a discipline support room immediately. (Use senior teacher back up for this.) Make sure the situation is resolved before you allow those particular students to join the next lesson (see Idea 56). Failure to respond firmly and quickly to this situation can have devastating results.

BULLYING IN THE CLASSROOM

The golden rule is do not, under any circumstances, be dragged into an argument with a student in the classroom. The fact that you're arguing with them shows that they have control of the situation. If you do make the mistake of arguing with the student this can easily ruin a lesson.

Instead, ask them to see you after the lesson and then focus straight back to the work in hand. If the student persists (and they often will) calmly repeat that you will not argue in the classroom. Be very firm. In most cases this will solve the problem as the student will realize that their ploy to disrupt has failed. But, if the student persists in an argument after all reasonable steps have been taken, then you must arrange to have that student removed immediately (see Idea 65).

THE GOLDEN RULE ABOUT DISAGREEMENTS

You will find that one big problem with the behaviour of students is to stop them talking about things which are not part of the lesson. (These are 'aliens'.) They will also often ask you questions about matters quite unrelated to the lesson. There will be a whole host of things which rear up which, often interesting in themselves, are unrelated to your lesson.

Also, they will be aware of the teacher's pet subject and they can be clever in bringing this up in order to avoid working.

How do you deal with this? If you keep dismissing them you can come over as very rigid and inflexible. This stance, in itself, does not make for good behaviour management. On the other hand, if you give in and engage in all sorts of chatter you can end up wasting loads of the lesson time.

There is a compromise which I have found works wonders. You defer requests for chat and questions and you say: 'Look, we can't discuss this now because we've got so much to get through in this lesson. [Of course, point to your lesson summary on the board!] However, if we make good progress we'll discuss these things in the special time!'

You will find that most students are happy to go along with this. Then, just before the end of the lesson, when everything is collected in and sorted out announce: 'Right, we can now have a bit of special time, as promised.' You can then discuss the deferred items. You will also find that it is a good way of ending a lesson.

A note of care. Be careful to plan the lesson carefully so that you can fit the special time in at the end. If you forget, or plan the time badly, it can cause bad feelings.

Also I have found it to be of great assistance to jot a couple of items to talk about on the board and write 'to be discussed in special time' next to them. To prevent too many being entered on the board say: 'Look, we'll see how we get on with those ones and if we have time we'll add some more.'

Like so many things in teaching, by achieving a workable compromise you can win through.

Everybody likes a bargain. You can use this fact to great effect when trying to encourage students to work. If they are not getting on with it, or have stopped working, you can suggest a smaller, easier task for them to do. Or you could offer to cancel a detention.

If applied with firm humour this method will produce great cooperation. For this to work well, have quiet conversations with individual students. A word of warning – don't be too easy to negotiate with!

THE POWER OF THE 'BARGAIN'

MOVING STUDENTS

Moving students can present problems. You ask a student to move and they refuse. What do you do? The whole class is watching. Do you get into an argument that you may well lose? First of all refer to 'The golden rules of seating plans' (Idea 105).

Here is what to do. Make sure the student has had several warnings. If, however, he or she continues to ignore your requests, walk over to the seat you want him or her to move to and pull it away from the desk. Then walk over to the student and hold one open hand towards him or her (with a distance of about half a metre), with the other hand pointing to the other seat and repeat your request. Then wait, remembering to stay calm. The student at this point may argue with you, however simply repeat your instructions, this time adding: 'I'm trying to get on with teaching my class; you're holding me up. I'm waiting.' Be calm and keep your voice low and firm.

If he or she still doesn't move then repeat the instructions. It's surprising how often a student will actually move at this point. There is strong psychological pressure at work here. In the rare cases when the student still won't move, then say: 'Right, I'm not wasting any more time with this. I will see you at the end of this lesson. I need to continue teaching my class.' Continue teaching and make sure you do see the student at the end and that a sanction is given, for example time out from the next lesson.

A big problem with students with challenging behaviour is their insistence on not wearing the school uniform correctly. You can choose to ignore it, although this could make the situation worse. Or you can choose to challenge the students and end up with arguments and serious disruption at the start of a lesson. So what do you do?

A good idea is to make the request to the whole class. As the lesson progresses carry on doing what you have planned but give reminders to the students who are still ignoring your instructions regarding the uniform. Make those reminders 'slip in' with the teaching but don't make them confrontational. After ten or 15 minutes, take out a notebook and say: 'Right, I'm not going to spend all lesson being ignored about the uniform. Those who are still ignoring me will have their names written in this book and you'll be dealt with by the head of year.'

Then begin to write their names in the book. You will be pleasantly surprised at how many will now comply with the uniform code. For those who still do not, have a quiet little mention to them at the end of the lesson and make sure that the head of year follows up with the school's sanction for incorrect dress code. If the student does not comply in the next lesson you'll have to arrange to have him or her isolated from your next lesson. It is a good idea to tell the class why this is being done. In this way the other students see that you mean what you say.

UNIFORM

MOBILE PHONES

This is a very common distraction for students. Check the guidelines your school has set down regarding mobile phones and make sure you are consistent in following them.

It can be very difficult to take phones from students. Try walking up to them, putting your hand out and asking politely but firmly for the phone. The student will go through the motions of putting the phone away. But it will come back a few seconds later. So you wait and then repeat your request but add that you'll put it in the cupboard and show the key for emphasis. There is something about this approach which makes the student think you really mean business. Although they may not hand you the phone you will find that it will not come out again.

It may be useful to refer back to Idea 20 here, as it asks you to think in advance about your reactions to common problems such as this.

Some behaviour problems are caused by the perception students have of always doing the same thing in your lessons. If they feel they're heading towards a dreary routine lesson, they will be uninterested in what you have to say before they even get to you!

To counteract this, surprise students with variety. Below is a sample of some of the many things you can try:

- go to the back of the room to talk to them so that they have to turn round;
- get them to stand up and gather around you as you show them a picture;
- have a TV programme playing on the video as they come in (it may be a theme connected to the lesson). Don't explain anything at the first stage just put a finger to your mouth and signal for them to sit quietly.
- hand them an envelope each as they come in which is sealed (it might have the starter in it) and hold a large card which says 'don't open it yet!';
- have a present wrapped up (a good idea is a bar of chocolate inside a big box covered in bright wrapping paper) which you hold up to show them and a sign which says: 'this present will be given to the quietest student at the end of the lesson!'

Variations will really command the attention of your students and get them looking forward to the next surprise in your lesson!

OVERCOMING THE RUT OF ROUTINES

'I HAVEN'T GOT A PEN'

This is so common and can be very irritating. If you have a ready supply of pens they soon disappear, and then where is the incentive for students to remember to bring a pen? On the other hand, not giving a spare pen can result in an even bigger problem as the student will use the absence of a pen to his or her full advantage to get out of doing any work.

A great idea is to have some pens ready with bright sticky tape on them in various colours. Make a point of reminding the student you'll need a word after the others have gone, and write the name of the student and the colour of the spare pen on the board. This ensures two things: first, you get your pen back and second, you've made your point and kept the flow of the lesson going without the student getting away with it.

It takes a small amount of preparation but this simple idea will bring a smooth solution to this common problem.

'We've already done this!' is another common phrase. This one can unnerve teachers quite easily. You must remain calm and not look surprised. Do not argue about whether or not they have done this particular piece of work before. Instead you can claim several very good reasons for repeating work. I've listed a few below.

○ You're looking at the same topic but from a different angle.
○ It's a very large topic and so a lot of time needs to be spent on it.
○ It's a difficult concept and so needs to be done more than once.
○ It's revision.

IDEA

79

'I'M NOT FEELING WELL!'

'I'm not feeling well!' is a tricky phrase to deal with. Monitor the situation carefully to see how the student is as the lesson progresses. You have to use your professional judgement to decide how genuine the case is. If they will not work after ten minutes, tell him or her that either they work or they must go to the medical room.

Sometimes a student will refer to another teacher regarding work they're doing in another class. Be very careful here. The student may criticize the teacher and try to goad you into agreeing. You must act decisively. Make a comment like: 'It is unprofessional to discuss other members of staff' and direct attention back to the task in hand. In most cases this will stop the problem.

If the student persists then you must treat it as a clear disciplinary matter. Remind the student more firmly that it is extremely impolite to continue with such comments and if necessary have the student removed from the room. In practice it is rare for it to reach this stage.

TALKING ABOUT ANOTHER TEACHER

IDEA 81

THE TEENAGE 'CRUSH'

It is a strange fact that students can develop a 'crush' on a teacher. You must be sensitive about this and usually after a short time it will pass. However, maintain meticulous professional conduct and if the student hangs around to speak to you on a regular basis for no apparent reason then arrange for another teacher to speak to them. If the student writes a personal note to you, whatever the content, it must be immediately referred to your line manager. Continue to treat the student as you normally would until the crush disappears.

If a student makes an abusive comment to you in the street, never deal with it there and then. Take it up next time you're at school with senior teachers.

The best way to deal with it is to arrange an early meeting to stop the situation getting out of control. The meeting should be with you, the senior teacher, the student and his or her parents or guardians. It must be explained that the matter is very serious. The school's ethos about polite behaviour extends outside the school as well. It must be made clear to the student that further abusive comments in the street will not be tolerated under any circumstances.

Make a file note of the incident for the record. It is best to end the meeting with a tone of forgiveness and reconciliation. Continue to treat the student as you would have done and make no further reference to the incident.

If, in rare cases, the abusive behaviour continues in the street rely on the school's system. Never try to deal with it as an individual.

ABUSIVE COMMENTS IN THE STREET

Giving out sanctions and rewards

THE DETENTION LETTER

Very often a teacher, frustrated with a student's behaviour, will resort to issuing a detention. That seems straightforward enough, however there are at least five major drawbacks to giving a detention.

1 It can often cause resentment immediately and make the situation worse.
2 You are involved in a round of form filling which can take up a lot of valuable time.
3 You must go through the follow-up process of checking that the student attended the detention (it is quite common for the student not to turn up).
4 If the student doesn't turn up then you either have to ignore it, in which case the whole system falls down, or get involved in yet more administration work reappointing the detention.
5 Detentions are often a cause of arguments with parents.

I am not suggesting for one moment that the detention system should be scrapped. As a last resort it can be an extremely useful sanction. There is however a better way to deal with things. Try having a 'formal detention warning' letter (as laid out opposite) as a buffer before entering the detention zone.

> The 'Formal Detention Warning' letter
> 'Despite reminders from the teacher to keep
> to the school rules the conduct of
>
> _____
>
> has continued to be un-cooperative. Notice
> is hereby given that if the situation of non-
> cooperation continues arrangements will be put
> in place for a detention in Room _____
> on _____.
>
> (Signed by the teacher)
> copies to Head of Department.'

I always make a big deal when I issue one of these.
Write the student's name in a book checking with
them who their form tutor is and then you hand
them the warning.

I have found that this works wonders. Students like
to have 'an escape route' and you will find that
often, after initial protests, the student's behaviour
will improve, and they will be anxious to confirm
with you that their behaviour is better by the end
of the lesson. The beauty of the idea is that it
involves the teacher in minimal work compared to
a detention and yet it produces better results.

TARGETING THE RINGLEADERS

It is tempting to react to a really bad lesson by punishing the whole class; after all it seemed like the whole class messed about. This is always a mistake. Instead, discern who the ringleaders are and make sure you only punish them. In a class of 25 you may find about five or seven ringleaders. It is not an exact science, but as a rule of thumb an average class of challenging behaviour will have a third who are comparatively easy to manage, a third who will mess around given the right conditions and a hardcore third of ringleaders.

I have observed new teachers with challenging classes. As their control of the class comes under threat they issue lots of sanctions. It can quickly escalate, which is a horrible experience, as you begin to wonder what on earth you can do to make it stop. Thoughts of cleaning windows for a job become a vision of heaven at these times!

I have found that the 'ladder of consequences' works extremely well. For example, if a particular group of students is misbehaving you can say: 'Right, in a moment I'm afraid I am going to consider moving one of you.' Notice that all you are actually threatening is 'to consider' something. However, it's the teacher's tone of voice which sends strong psychological messages to the class as a whole. You are not going to lose face or be involved in the arguments which the giving of detentions can generate.

At the point when a sanction becomes necessary say: 'You leave me no choice, Martin, I'm writing your name in my book.' Notice that you're simply writing a name in a book! The written word seems to carry great authority and power. You put the book back into your pocket and direct attention straight back on to the lesson.

To sum up, don't give your most severe punishment first. Use a strong tone of voice, always direct attention back to the work and increase your threats slowly.

THE 'LADDER OF CONSEQUENCES'

When you're trying to settle a class it's tempting to always say negative things. The problem with this is that it sets up a confrontational atmosphere that almost always invites bad behaviour.

A better approach is to tell them off with praise. For example: 'Michael, you're the last person I would have thought would interrupt me, you normally listen so well.' If used carefully this will have a far better outcome.

PRAISING STUDENTS

Try motivating your challenging group by organizing a weekly raffle. The prize could be a bar of chocolate or a magic trick box (anything you think they'll like!). To be entered the students must maintain a good behaviour level throughout the week. You'll be surprised how well this works as students start to behave so as not to miss out on the fun.

You can add to the effectiveness by making little 'deals' where you agree to put their name back in the draw if they improve their behaviour straight away. It also creates a bit of welcome fun at the end of the week and helps foster better longer-term relationships between you and your students.

THE RAFFLE

THE PROPORTIONAL PUNISHMENT

Try to make sure that a punishment is proportional to the behaviour that led to it. For example, if you catch a student damaging your wall display, arrange for a short detention for him or her to come to your room and repair it. The student will see this as a fair consequence.

If a student is particularly unkind to another student then arrange for the student causing the problem to stay back for a short while to write a letter of apology. If a student forgets to bring in homework for a second time arrange for a lunchtime detention in which the student can complete the work. If, however, there is a serious problem, for example violent behaviour, then make sure that parents are brought into the school to urgently discuss the matter with a senior member of staff. If the students see that generally the punishment and response is fair and proportional the whole discipline system will work more efficiently and effectively.

Teaching is a long-term engagement and the development of consistent and effective habits will make your job easier. One is to build good relationships with your students. It is good to say things like: 'You're a pleasant lad; however, when you call out like that you're ignoring the school's rules. Please sort that out.' That is a far better way to reprimand a student than to say: 'You're always calling out. You're very annoying.'

As teachers we shouldn't forget that students' feelings work exactly like ours do as adults. If somebody criticizes us we naturally get defensive and it's no different for them.

Even when you need to give a serious sanction, like a detention, you can say

> *'It really is a shame Matthew. Most of the time you are fine, but that last lesson you decided to ignore all my instructions. Therefore you must do this detention, and then next lesson we'll get you back to normal.'*

In this way, the students will see that you're being fair in doing your job. This is a vital tip and will help you succeed in the long run.

SEPARATING THE BEHAVIOUR FROM THE STUDENT

GIVING REWARDS

Have a supply of congratulation letters typed out on headed paper with a space for the student's name and a box to handwrite the specific area of work being praised. This means that the letter can be quickly written out in the lesson and handed to the student there and then. The immediacy of this reward makes it very effective. You can also say at the start of the lesson: 'Now, I have three letters to go home to praise you. Who is going to earn them?' This sets a challenge. Keep the letters to about three per lesson for maximum effect. Too many will devalue them.

A great way to show that you appreciate the efforts of your students is to over-reward them. Exceed their expectations!

If you have promised them a bronze certificate make it up to a silver one! Tell them that you have thought about their efforts and you are so pleased you have decided to increase their reward.

It doesn't really matter what the reward is. The main point is that you give them more than they expected. You exceed your promise. When you do this there is powerful psychology at work. They will appreciate the feeling that they have made a huge gain. They will feel encouraged to work that bit harder next time.

But be strategic about this. If students expect you routinely to put up your reward then it will lose its effect. The thing to do is mainly and mostly keep to the rewards you say, but, occasionally and strategically (where you think it will encourage most effectively), exceed your promise.

It has another benefit. Students get to know that you always at least keep to your promise and it brings your reward system to life as the students will feel that someone is going to get more than they thought, maybe! It just makes it all more fun.

BRING REWARDS ALIVE

THE VIDEO TREAT

Try to keep the treat of showing a video to a minimum. If shown at the end of term, or after a difficult unit of work, then it makes it appear more of a treat. If you have a selection of videos it's best not to ask the class which one they want. All this will do is cause an argument that could wreck your lesson. Instead, carefully choose one which you think they'll like (the more up to date the better) and just put it straight on. There will be protestors but they'll settle down.

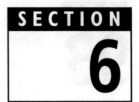

The big picture

THE GOLDEN HABIT OF TEACHING

There really are two ways in which you can tackle the problem of behaviour management.

You can struggle along with what seems to work and repeat your actions time and time again. You will see yourself battling with a 'difficult' job and that the problems you have are down to the difficult group you teach. Many teachers carry on like this for years. The problem with this is that, although you'll get the job done, you'll feel that teaching is full of unavoidable drudgery. This type of teacher never has time to step back and look at how he's doing.

There is another way. This is where you constantly think about how you could improve your behaviour management techniques. To do this you should

○ reflect on behavioural issues that arise in your lessons. Ask yourself this question: 'How could I have handled that better?'
○ consult with other teachers and ask them how they handled similar situations
○ read all there is to read about the subject of behaviour management and go on any courses you can or else watch training videos
○ trial run different behaviour-management techniques to see what works best for you

With this habit of constant reflection and improvement you will notice yourself becoming better at controlling your class and as a result you will enjoy teaching more and more. What is more the students will learn more and respect you for your skills.

Therefore, make it a priority to be the type of teacher who constantly learns and improves. Set aside a bit of time each day for this as if you were setting time aside to eat or drink.

An assembly is not just another lesson. It is a grouping of a large number of people together in one place and the situation requires special handling.

I have seen many assemblies which have gone horribly wrong. It often comes down to the teacher trying to improvise! Many a competent teacher has walked up to the stage and delivered a spur of the moment assembly. It starts off all right but then runs out of steam.

The key thing is to practise, practise, practise! Start off with your idea, develop it, add interesting examples, deploy techniques for holding the attention of a large crowd (see below) and run it through several times before you deliver it.

Don't make it interactive! I have seen teachers casually ask questions of the students like: 'Who saw the football last night?' In the face of the ensuing mayhem they have bravely carried on above the noise with comments like 'Good, wasn't it?' and smiled and nodded to someone on the front row. Then the teacher gets suddenly angry about the noise and starts shouting for quiet. What a disaster! By this time the hundreds of students who are talking about the football are a formidable lot to suddenly quieten down. But it is quiet you must have to make a good assembly.

When the correct techniques are deployed and the assembly is delivered in an interesting way to the students, then a certain wonderful magic will appear. This is the same magic created every night in a theatre when a large group of people listen with silent interest to one person speaking.

Make yourself an expert at delivering great assemblies and it will help you enormously with your skill at behaviour management generally.

MAKING AN ASSEMBLY A SUCCESS

Here are some of the best techniques which have been useful to me over the years:

1 Stand still for most of the time. If you move, do so for dramatic effect. Keep hand gestures to a minimum.

2 Never read your presentation. Have key points written on small hand-held cards and discreetly glance at them.

3 Look at your audience and scan them as much as you can. Do not stare at one person or look at the wall at the back.

4 Use dramatic pauses. Let the effect of what you say sink in. Repeat key points to create impact. Repeat key phrases slowly and quietly and then pause and look at your audience. Allow silence to work for you.

5 Stay relaxed. Think before you speak. Sometimes deliver slowly, sometimes speed up. Sometimes speak softly and now and then raise the volume. Variety destroys boredom.

6 Keep your vocabulary simple and use stress to emphasize certain words.

7 Use the 'magic three' to give impact to what you say. For example: 'Don't drop litter today; don't drop litter tomorrow; never drop litter!'

8 Use analogies, metaphors and similes to bring your talking alive. For example: don't say 'We're moving up the league table', instead say: 'Imagine a ladder leaning against a house. We were on the bottom rung looking at the mud; now, we're halfway up and we have the roof in sight!'

9 Use rhetorical questions sparingly, otherwise some students will try to shout an answer.

10 Make your message clear by structuring it, using the age-old method: tell them at the start what you're going to tell them; tell them in the middle

what the main message is; tell them at the end what you have told them.

11 Finish with something which is rousing and memorable. For example, if it's about litter say: 'So if each student does their bit today and picks up litter, just think how clean and tidy our school will be tomorrow when younger brothers and sisters come here!'

One last point – don't say: 'I'm going to tell you a story.' There is something about the word 'story' which reminds them of long drawn-out, boring experiences. You will see some of them adversely react to that word. Instead say something like: 'I'd like to share something fascinating with you now.'

Most teachers will be called upon to invigilate exams from time to time and it is surprising how a great deal of trouble can be avoided by following certain guidelines. You need to give invigilation special consideration because the exams are controlled by outside organizations. If things go wrong, even seemingly little things, it can cause a lot of trouble.

The main thing is to prepare carefully. Check

o exactly when and where you are required (make sure you get the invigilation schedule well in advance)
o if materials are required
o if any special arrangements are needed

Go to the person responsible for that particular exam and double-check the arrangements. It is best to be very pedantic about this. You'll find that very often little things are overlooked and need to be sorted. A typical example could be books required for the exam are locked in a cupboard and the key is missing. By planning carefully in advance you will be one step ahead of foreseeable problems.

Make sure that you have read and studied, in advance, every detail of the 'Rules for Examinations' issued by the Examinations Board. In the heat of the exam there are high levels of stress and certainly no time to wade through small print, finding out what is allowed and what is not. Don't rely on someone else knowing.

Chat through with your fellow invigilators, before the exam, how you intend to give out and collect up materials. This sounds obvious but will help the smooth flow of proceedings at the time. Check out how the register will be taken. It is off-putting for the candidates to have their concentration interrupted as a teacher moves their paper to read their name card. Keep from talking to other teachers during the exam unless it is for urgent and unavoidable things. Teachers find it hard not to talk but the candidates must not be disturbed.

Check that your own mobile phone is switched off. This can save huge embarrassment!

If there are behaviour problems during the exam make sure that you know the school's policy for dealing with them in every detail. Usually it involves a quiet word to the candidate, but if the problem persists there must be senior support, at hand, to deal with it swiftly. The consequences of not knowing in advance what to do, or not having someone to call on when you need them, can be disastrous! It is not like a lesson. These candidates have a right to uninterrupted concentration and this must remain at the centre of your care in handling invigilation.

Make sure that all papers and materials are carefully collected before dismissal. Be careful as to where the papers are put! They must be taken immediately to the examinations officer after the exam.

Take care with dismissal. Insist on a row by row approach otherwise you will have chaos.

One last thing. It seems a very obvious thing, but I can't forget that many years ago a teacher I knew handed out the wrong papers and only discovered the mistake halfway through the exam. The trouble which this caused had very far-reaching effects!

SURVIVING A COVER LESSON

A lot of teachers dread cover lessons. If problems are going to happen that is where they will most likely be. The fact about cover lessons is that they are an important part of your teacher contract and if you can take steps to make yourself more efficient in that area then you will lower your overall stress and further enhance your skills at dealing with behaviour management.

So what are the main problems routinely encountered with a cover lesson? Most teachers would say:

○ unknown class who will play up more with a cover teacher
○ no seating plan
○ not knowing their names
○ unfamiliar room and logistic problems arising from that – for example, where is the key to the door?
○ work not set
○ materials required are not to hand
○ not being an expert on the subject
○ being unsure of the discipline support back-up system for that particular department
○ unaware of the group's routines

Here are some suggested ideas to improve your cover lesson experience:

If you know that tomorrow you are 'at risk' of being asked to provide cover, don't wait until it happens but ask the cover manager today if you can have advance notice of who you have to cover for. Although you will not know for sure who is off until the next day it is surprising how often you can be asked to cover for a teacher who has booked absence sometimes weeks in advance. The cover manager may well be able to pencil you in the night before. If you do know in advance it will give you time to pop round and check where the room is, who has the key and what the materials are. You may even be able to get the cover work in advance to allow you some extra time to look at it and prepare things.

Whether or not you know in advance there are certain things you can do to help yourself in any case. Find out what the discipline-support arrangements are for each department and faculty by chatting with the head of each section. This is a vital thing to do. Beware! If you are faced with a student you do not know in your cover lesson, who badly plays up and you do not know the efficient way to have him removed, that experience can take its place among the worst you will ever have in teaching!

Make sure that you carry with you a 'survival package' of spare pens, paper, board pens, tissues, etc.

Try to get a seating plan in advance. If you can't, make sure that during the lesson you produce a seating plan so that you can use their names. A good way to do this is to ask a reliable-looking student to tell you discreetly who everyone is.

So the main message with cover lessons is: don't treat them as low priority and as a nuisance just to get out the way. It is part of your contract, so prepare conscientiously and you will find that it greatly enhances the experience.

Every teacher I've ever met has a passion for something (often many things). Why not take a bit of time to harness this rich resource for the benefit of teachers and students by forming an 'expert presentation club'?

Each teacher involved prepares a presentation based on their particular passion and expert knowledge. It can be arranged within the department or across departments and doesn't need to be curriculum-based.

The next step is to work out a timetable of presentations. Free periods can be used to minimize disruption to the timetable. You then present to each other's classes.

Although it appears a shame in the short term to give up a treasured free period it has major advantages:

○ teachers love to show off their passion given the right conditions. They seem to go into another 'gear'
○ the students' learning is enhanced and enriched by having someone different in their classroom. Their behaviour will be improved by this experience
○ it engenders teamwork among colleagues and is good fun
○ it allows you to observe other teachers' techniques to add ideas to your own armoury
○ it is nice to enrich the syllabus occasionally rather than always sticking precisely to it
○ it is something which, once set up, can be developed, refined and reused

A fantastic way to build great relationships with the students which also translates into better behaviour management is to start an 'after-school club'.

Have it on the same day each week and start it 15 minutes after the end of school for, say, 30–45 minutes. Constantly remind students about it and talk it up.

The purpose of the club is to give extra help and encouragement but make it fun. Have things to eat and drink, play music and keep the atmosphere relaxed.

I know that a lot of teachers scoff at such an idea and believe that such a club only works with well-behaved students. But if you try it out, organize it well, keep it going and have clear ground rules you'll find that a few students will come, and if they enjoy it, will get others to come. With students with challenging behaviour you can give more one-to-one individual help. The results can be truly amazing.

It is another way of showing the students you care and I have often had students show great disappointment when such a club is discontinued. Remember, for some of them the prospect of going home is not always that great.

AFTER-SCHOOL CLUBS

IDEA
99

Teaching assistants (TAs) are a fantastically useful resource in helping to deal with bad behaviour. Unfortunately, due to time restraints and all sorts of other reasons, it's common to find that TAs are not used effectively at all. It is important for a good strong professional bond to be established between you and your TA. Below are some golden rules to developing an effective partnership.

o Make time to meet outside of the lesson to briefly outline strategies and approaches.

o Develop a double act by rehearsing a set of 'what ifs' so that together you will have more confidence in your approach.

o Don't forget to give your assistant a thumbnail outline of the lesson plan.

o Allow and encourage your assistant to have the full authority for discipline that you have, and constantly remind your class of this.

o If you have a particularly challenging student you may wish to sit your assistant next to that student to help focus him or her on to his or her work.

o If you are reading to the class or demonstrating something, it's a good idea to get your TA to help with this as it's more interesting for the students to hear another voice and (not to mention) more interesting for the assistant too.

o So with a little bit of planning and discussion you can develop a partnership with your assistant which will bring huge rewards when dealing with challenging behaviour.

Often with a challenging class teachers feel, quite naturally, that it's too risky to bring in a visitor. However, a fantastic way to help a challenging class is to actively arrange for other people to come in and do a presentation. For example: poets, folk singers, adventurers, professionals talking about their jobs, retired people reflecting on their lives, experts on a particular subject (e.g. UFOs), and so on. As you get more established at your school you can build up a network of contacts. The contacts can be local or people within the school.

There's something about the sense of occasion and the presence of the visitor in the room that really raises interest levels. Students always enjoy the surprise of someone new and you can be creative and inventive with the way you link the visitor to the work you're currently doing.

People are very often flattered to be asked and will spend a great deal of time and effort preparing without expecting anything in return other than the experience of presenting their topic. Often they will bring in things to display that raise the interest level of students even further. The main thing to bear in mind is to plan ahead and give your guest plenty of time to prepare in advance.

Why not also try involving members of the support staff? You may find, for example, that the head caretaker has been on a trip to Australia and has plenty to talk about on the different culture, cuisine and animals out there.

ENHANCING THE VISITING SPEAKER

More and more schools are inviting in guest speakers and experts in their field to give presentations to the students. This is a great thing but there can be a particular problem in this area.

Usually the teacher will introduce the speaker and hand over to him and he will naturally deliver his presentation. Most often, however, and as expected, the speaker will not have the experience and skill of a teacher which is required to manage the students' behaviour. This puts the teacher in an awkward position because he stands on the sideline, watching passively because he doesn't want to interrupt and intrude on the presentation. The students know this. Their behaviour can often change (for the worse) and the speaker is either unaware, unwilling or unable to manage the behaviour. Often the situation deteriorates until the teacher is forced to intervene, usually with a lot of shouting, and the situation quickly becomes wholly unsatisfactory.

A good solution to this is to arrange a 'double act' with the speaker in advance of the presentation. Yes, the speaker will deliver their particular knowledge in their particular way but the teacher will have an active role in assisting the presentation. For example, he may hold up an exhibit or point to things on a board or read something out. The advantage is that the teacher's active presence helps manage the behaviour and he can more easily make things run smoothly by actively commenting to the students. Because he is part of the presentation his assistance in the management of their behaviour seems much more natural. As far as the delivery of the skills or knowledge goes then the focus is of course on the speaker.

A few minutes' planning in advance along these lines with the speaker will enhance the experience for everyone. I have found that the invited speaker usually welcomes this suggestion and it makes everyone more comfortable.

One of the really pleasant surprises in teaching is that the vast majority of parents and guardians will support the teacher in his or her efforts in dealing with challenging behaviour. The important thing to remember is to ask specifically for their support. A lot of teachers wait until parents' consultation day. The problem with this is that often you'll find the very parents you want to speak to will not be there.

If you experience challenging behaviour and it doesn't improve in response to your normal strategies, then phone the parents promptly. Time spent on this now will pay huge dividends in the future management of the problem. It helps if you can be very specific and play up the positive aspect. For example: 'Dean is on Level 4 and we are trying to get him to Level 5. He is nearly there.'

Outline the ways in which you've tried to tackle the problem, and remember to be careful with your words, as however badly behaved the child is, he or she is a precious treasure to the parent! Then ask for help from the parent. You might say: 'I think that we're agreed that we both want Dean to do well in his work. Could you think of anything that you could do that might reinforce my efforts?' In most cases the parent will be able to suggest a sanction that they can give at home to support you. At the end of the conversation don't forget to sum up what has been agreed like this:

> 'So Mrs Smith, I do appreciate your time with this. Just to confirm then, if Dean doesn't respond to reasonable requests to behave himself then you will consider keeping him at home in the evenings for up to a week. That's great. Thank you.'

This is a powerful advantage if you take the time to set it up.

I find it a useful and an even more powerful advantage if I confirm the conversation with parents in writing straight away, and then keep in contact with the parent until things improve. Then you can both celebrate the improvement which has been achieved.

A further point is to mention your arrangement with their parents in an encouraging way to the student without the rest of the class hearing. I find the end of the lesson as the others leave the room is a good time to mention it briefly. Say something like: 'Dean, I've spoken to your mum and she, like me, wants you to do well. I hope that by the end of this week we can send a letter to say that things are improving!' Keep it to that. Don't mention what the sanction is as this will lead to conflict.

If this is carefully organized and followed up consistently, it will result in a huge improvement to the situation.

CONFIRMING PARENTAL AGREEMENTS

How you set out your classroom has a vital impact on the control of your students' behaviour. Below are my golden rules:

○ make sure that with challenging students they're all seated facing your way;
○ if the group is small enough insist on one to a double desk;
○ keep ringleaders apart;
○ have enough space so that you can get to each desk easily;
○ make sure there is plenty of space between the board and the front row of desks;
○ keep areas around your cupboard and desk clear for ease of access;
○ make sure everything you need is to hand.

If you make sure these simple things are in place it will make your lesson much easier to manage.

Seating plans are an absolute necessity when dealing with a challenging group. Here are my golden rules.

1 When initially preparing the seating plan, make sure the seats are laid out as you want them. Keep the more demanding students away from each other. Make sure that special needs are catered for. For example, a student with poor eyesight will need to be at the front.

2 If the group is small enough, insist on one student per double desk.

3 Ensure that the first few lessons are successful in getting students to sit at their allocated places. If it requires senior teacher assistance to enforce this in the early stages then so be it. This is a battle that must be won. It is better that students are taken out of the class than to allow them to sit where they wish.

4 Have copies of the seating plan typed up. You can have an enlarged copy put up on the wall with the name of the class boldly above it.

The students will ask to move and this can seem innocent enough. A vast variety of reasons are offered. At all costs resist the request to move seat. If you agree to one move I assure you that you will find a case of 'musical chairs' each lesson and the situation will worsen. In the end the students will sit wherever they please. Be cruel to be kind.

THE GOLDEN RULES OF SEATING PLANS

If a student gets out of his or her seat without permission make sure you ask him or her to return to it immediately. Absolutely insist that the students stay in their seats during a lesson. Reinforce this all the time. It is amazing how much trouble and disruption can be traced back to students leaving their seats when they please.

There is no reason why a student should need to get up without permission. If for example, it's to sharpen a pencil, sharpen it for them. Alongside this, make sure you have excellent systems for handing out and collecting in work to minimize the need for students to wander about (for tips on this see Idea 28).

KEEPING STUDENTS IN THEIR SEATS

Now and again it's necessary to move a group from one room to another. This could be to use the library or a computer room. In the case of a very challenging group there is one golden rule: don't do it!

If it's unavoidable that you use another room then it should be arranged in advance and the students need to be told to go to the new room instead of the old room for the next lesson. Have the door to the old room locked at the beginning of the lesson and arrange assistance. You will need to be stationed at the new room and another teacher must be outside the locked door of the old room reminding students where they should be. It's a good idea never to have a lesson which starts in one room and then is moved to another.

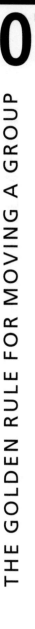

THE GOLDEN RULE FOR MOVING A GROUP

FREEING TIME

With the management of behaviour the more time you can free up to spend on preparing the better. Marking books takes a great portion of a teacher's time and this idea is designed to free up a significant amount of time for you.

You will find that with any subject the marking of books requires you to write the same sorts of comments repeatedly. Obviously not all the comments are repeated but a surprisingly large proportion of them are.

The solution is to produce your own stickers. You can buy sheets of stickers and 21 to an A4 sheet is about the best size. You can program your computer to print stickers and you can prepare a whole set of them with regularly used comments. To enhance them you can add pictures and so on.

You will find that an initial investment of time will set you up with a great time-saving idea. I find that it helps to organize the stickers into folders. Different types of comments can be colour-coded in different ways.

I have found that once the system is up and running it can save you approximately 35 per cent of marking time and the presentation in the books is so much more professional.

This is a very basic point but it's amazing how many teachers forget to comply with it. If you're telling off or praising a student at the end of the lesson when the rest of the class have gone, you must always have another student, teacher or teaching assistant in the room with you. This is common sense and must not be forgotten. In the absolute vast majority of cases it will be unnecessary, but it must be done to protect you against the potential of a false allegation of misconduct.

BEING ALONE WITH A STUDENT

REMINDING THEM OF THE REASONS FOR GOOD BEHAVIOUR

Rather than school being teachers versus students it should be that teachers and students work together to progress with the work. This is the underlying philosophy behind the ideas in this book.

It is a good idea to frequently remind students about why you're asking them to stick to the protocols. This helps in getting them to comply because they see the sense in it, rather than just being told what to do. It also helps to show that you really are on their side.

SECTION

7

Managing yourself

THE TWO TIMETABLES

It is easy to stick to the school timetable. However, a lot of teachers work long hours on preparation, marking, etc. In the long run this will wear you down. So it's a good idea to make a second timetable for your work outside of classroom hours.

It works particularly well if you take specific jobs, for example marking, preparing lessons, administration and anything unexpected, and allocate them specific times. For example: Mondays 4–5pm – mark Year 8 exercise books; Tuesdays 4–5pm – do all outstanding admin work, and so on.

The main advantage to this system is that if you're meticulous and stick to it, any potential worry is removed and your spare time is freed up for you to enjoy yourself and recharge your batteries.

You cannot predict all the tasks that you do but if you keep a good record of how you spend your time over a period of a month it helps you to plan accurately and allocate tasks for future planning.

An important part of this arrangement is to be tough on yourself. If you have a set of books to mark in one hour then divide up the time by the amount of books and spend a certain amount of time on each book and no more. Otherwise a job has a habit of expanding to fill more time than it should.

It is a horrible experience to go to bed feeling that important tasks remain unfinished and with a sense of confusion about what must be done first. The idea for the 'second timetable' takes away this horrible experience and replaces it with a sense of being in control of your time, work and life.

You will never get everything done – ask any teacher! So, to help with organizing your priorities make a list of things to do under three headings:

A Must do.
B Should do.
C Would be nice to do.

Group the tasks into categories. For example, marking; planning; preparation of lessons; preparation of resources; and administration.

Make sure that you have a clear idea of the minimum requirements for the job and a clear view of your 'job description'. It is a good idea at this stage to get an experienced teacher in your subject area to look at your list and comment on it. Then make sure that all the minimum requirements of your job are marked with an 'A' category. Once category 'A' items are done then, and only then, do category 'B' items and then category 'C' items.

PRIORITIES

IDEA

113

Watch any teacher and you'll see them burning adrenalin like rocket fuel. So, on a daily basis make an appointment with yourself to relax. Ask your family not to disturb you. Once it becomes a habit stick to it come what may.

It might also be a good idea to go to relaxation classes to learn techniques about how to relax. And difficult though it is, cut down on tea and coffee and substitute with fruit juice and water. I find this greatly helps relaxation.

It is particularly important in teaching to become an expert on relaxation techniques during your working day. Many teachers are always on edge and this puts the students on edge.

Here are a couple of simple techniques which work very well:

o clench your fists tightly for a count of seven and then relax them. Repeat this a few times and feel the tension ebb away;

o be conscious of your breathing and make it become deep, slow and steady. Just ten breaths of this sort can calm you;

o make sure you walk around as much as possible, in the classroom and between lessons. This is a great stress buster.

Choose a form of exercise and do it for one hour three times a week. No excuses! Your family will soon get used to your 'recharge' routine. I find the best types of exercise are those that are not fiercely competitive. For example: dancing, cycling, walking, swimming, golf and yoga.

Find the one that suits you and your lifestyle. The main thing to remember is to do regular small sessions that you can keep up the whole year round. That way you will get the best stress-busting benefit.

To encourage yourself, maintain a logbook of your exercise. Over time you'll find yourself trying to improve on your previous weekly total.

Slow and steady exercise works well. For example, you can learn tai chi. This exercise allows you to clear your mind, reduces muscle tension and gives you an enhanced sense of well-being.

Remember, whichever exercise you decide on, stick with it. The benefits to you and your job will be enormous.

EXERCISE

YOUR EVENING

Have one evening a week in which you do your own thing. This can be anything as long as it's not connected to work. I find a Friday is best. Giving your mind a rest is essential for stress relief and for promoting peace of mind. After a while you'll look forward to this special break for yourself. There is something about taking your mind off your job on a regular basis that is deeply satisfying. When you return to work you will feel more refreshed and balanced.

If you can get involved in something that has a social aspect, but with people who are not teachers, you will find that it broadens your horizons and allows you to see yourself in a wider perspective. It can be a refreshing break and good fun to regularly meet with a group where you share common interests.

By having one evening a week it can be regarded as a well-earned reward for working hard.

Why not join an evening class and learn something new? It is fantastic as a teacher to be able to cross the line and become a student. Psychologically it does you wonders and I've found that going to evening classes and discovering new subjects is a great joy.

Teachers are always giving out information and therefore it's good to have new information and ideas coming in. Another advantage to an evening class is that it develops your circle of friends to include those who are not teachers.

Another advantage is that you'll find your self-esteem increases as you learn new areas of knowledge. I particularly suggest joining a class where you learn something unusual or new to you. It is amazing how the new learning experience will activate parts of your mind that you forgot you had.

BECOMING A STUDENT AGAIN

SLOWING THE PACE

Teaching a class of demanding children has a profoundly draining effect on you. When you're in the classroom they're at you all the time. You have to be on your toes and on peak performance. Building on Ideas 113, 114 and 115, it's a good idea to make a conscious effort to slow down and ease any tension once outside the classroom. For example, slow your steps when you walk and think about the rhythm and pace of your breathing. When you eat, eat slowly, and remember to enjoy the food. When this turns into a lifestyle habit recharging your batteries will be so much easier!

To take away the guilt of not seeing friends as often as you should, schedule meeting them in the holidays and spread it out around the year. Your friends will soon get to know your reasons. I have known teachers who go through agonies trying to fit everyone in. While it's great to have colleagues who become friends, it's also good to keep in contact with friends who aren't teachers. You realize that there's more to life than just teaching issues!

FRIENDS

As you might not see your friends as much you'd like to, why not make the occasions when you do see them particularly special.

Some suggestions are:

○ paying Cluedo dressed up in character;
○ murder mystery events;
○ paintballing;
○ medieval banquets;
○ theatre trips;
○ general knowledge evenings.

They may take time to organize but the fun you'll have will give you pleasant memories for years!

A WARM BATH

Take a warm bath before you go to bed and read a light-hearted book. Even better is to light a candle and in the soft light listen to a favourite CD. Falling asleep will be so much easier.

A lot of teachers are so committed to their work that they work late into the evening. It is essential to have a cut-off time that you stick to. Plan your evening so that you do have time for a long relaxing soak in the bath.

Always remember that the more relaxed your evening is the more efficient you will be the next day. You will need that energy to tackle those challenging students!

Keep a daily record of what you have done in a simplified form. After school, spend a few minutes jotting down the main things you've accomplished. Include things you feel you've done well in.

Keep all appointments and plans in one diary, and all 'to do' items on one 'to do' list. The ideal situation is to have all this in the one notebook.

In teaching it is absolutely vital to be well organized. Make sure that all paperwork is carefully filed in a way in which you can find what you need quickly. It is well worth having a certain amount of time each day to keep your organization up to date.

IDEA

120

A SIMPLE WORK LOG